Big **BAD** Book of

BART SIMPSON

El Bart FOR CLASS PRESIDENT

Skinner is a jerk!

TITAN BOOKS

In memory of Dan DeCarlo:

Comic book legend, mentor, and friend.

The Simpsons™, created by Matt Groening, is the copyrighted
and trademarked property of Twentieth Century Fox Film Corporation.
Used with permission. All rights reserved.

BIG BAD BOOK OF BART SIMPSON

FIRST EDITION: JUNE 2003

ISBN 9781840236545
10 9

Publisher: MATT GROENING
Creative Director: BILL MORRISON
Managing Editor: TERRY DELEGEANE
Director of Operations: ROBERT ZAUGH
Special Projects Art Director: SERBAN CRISTESCU
Art Director: NATHAN KANE
Production Manager: CHRISTOPHER UNGAR
Legal Guardian: SUSAN A. GRODE

Trade Paperback Concepts and Design: SERBAN CRISTESCU

Contributing Artists:
IGOR BARANKO, KAREN BATES, JOHN COSTANZA, DAN DECARLO, MIKE DECARLO, LUIS ESCOBAR,
TIM HARKINS, CHIA-HSIEN JASON HO, NATHAN KANE, MIKE KAZALEH, CAROLYN KELLY, LEE
LOUGHRIDGE, SCOTT MCRAE, BILL MORRISON, KEVIN M. NEWMAN, PHYLLIS NOVIN, ANDREW PEPOY,
RICK REESE, MIKE ROTE, SCOTT SHAW!, STEVE STEERE, JR., ART VILLANUEVA, MIKE WORLEY
Contributing Writers:
JAMES BATES, TERRY DELEGEANE, CHUCK DIXON, GEORGE GLADIR, EARL KRESS, ERIC ROGERS,
SCOTT SHAW!, GAIL SIMONE, CHRIS YAMBAR

PRINTED IN SPAIN

TABLE OF CONTENTS

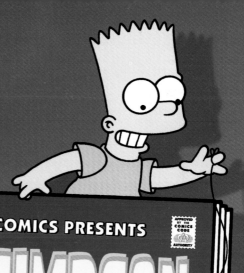

SIMPSONS COMICS PRESENTS

BART SIMPSON

★ MENACE TO SOCIETY ★

#5

US $2.50
CAN $3.50

WESTERN TERRITORY, 1872

THE WELLS ARE EMPTY...

...AND THE RIVERS AND CREEKBEDS HAVE RUN DRY.

GASP!

GASP!

CHOKE!

WILD, WILD BART

| GAIL "ANNIE OAKLEY" SIMONE SCRIPT | JOHN "JESSE JAMES" COSTANZA PENCILS | STEVE "BUTCH CASSIDY" STEERE, JR. INKS | LEE "SUNDANCE KID" LOUGHRIDGE COLORS | KAREN "CALAMITY JANE" BATES LETTERS | BILLY "THE KID" MORRISON EDITOR | MATT "BAT MASTERSON" GROENING BIG BOSS |

PLOK!

PLOK!

PLOK!

DR. RALPH BRANELESS. MARTIMUS, I *KNOW* THAT EVIL GENIUS IS AT THE BOTTOM OF THIS!

WILD WEST AIR HOCKEY

MARTIMUS? WHY, I'M SURE I DON'T KNOW *WHO* YOU MEAN! I'M *SHERRI*, THE DANCE HALL GIRL WITH THE HEART OF GOLD!

WILD WEST

AIR HOCKEY

NICE *TRY*, MARTIMUS.

DASH IT ALL, BART. YOU *ALWAYS* SEE THROUGH MY *CUNNING DISGUISES*!

6

NO TIME TO PLAY *DRESS-UP*, MARTIMUS. BRANELESS IS STEALIN' ALL THE *WATER* OUT OF THE WEST. EVERY LAKE AND RIVER IS DRYIN' UP!

WITHOUT *WATER*, EVERY LIVING THING IN THE WEST IS IN *DANGER*!

POP!

PLOK!

VULTURE'S GULCH

...AND *THIS* IS THE DIRTY, LOW-DOWN TOWN WHERE *BRANELESS* WAS LAST *SEEN*! SADDLE UP, MARTIMUS, WE'RE GOIN' *RIDIN'*!

A *CAPITAL* IDEA!

FASTER, MARTIMUS! PRESIDENT GRANT IS *DEPENDIN'* ON US!

I'M *CHAFING BADLY*, AND I'VE *SWALLOWED* A VARIETY OF *INSECTS*!

WELL, THIS IS THE PLACE!

OH, I *DO* HOPE THEY HAVE *PEPPERMINT JULEPS*!

VULTURE'S GULCH SODA SALOON & GIN RUMMY PARLOR

NO SHIRT, NO SPURS, NO SERVICE

OUTHOUSE FOR CUSTOMERS ONLY!

♪ CAMPTOWN LADIES, SING THIS SONG DO DAH, DO DAH! CAMPTOWN RACE TRACK FIVE MILES LONG, OH, ♪ THE DO DAH DAY! ♪

CAREEEEEK!

ROOT BEER

I'M HERE LOOKIN' FOR A SKUNK NAMED *BRANELESS*.

...AND I'D LIKE A *PEPPERMINT JULEP*, PLEASE!

MAYBE YA SHOULDN'T BE NOSIN' AROUND HERE, STRANGER. THE BOSS WOULDN'T *LIKE* IT!

WHOOOA! I'M *SO* SCARED! WHAT ARE YA GONNA DO, THROW YOUR *ROOT BEER* AT ME?

ER...BART, MAYBE WE SHOULD...

KEEERAASSHH!!!!

...DUCK!

AYE CABALLERO!*

*ED'S NOTE: A CABALLERO IS A SPANISH HORSEMAN!—BUFFALO BILL MORRISON

8

PLOK!

OLD MAID

S

SMASH!

U.S. SECRET SERVICE CHEWING GUM

DYNAMITE FLAVOR!

CAUTION: NOT HYPERBOLE! FLAVORED WITH REAL DYNAMIT

EXPLOSIVE! (REALLY! WE MEAN IT!)

BLAAMMO!

WELL, NOW WE JUST HAVE TO WAKE ONE OF THEM UP, AND HE'LL TAKE US *RIGHT TO DR. BRANELESS!*

HOW *HUMILIATING!*

BART! *LOOK OUT!*

KONNK!

UGNNHH!

WELL, STRANGER, I GUESS YOU DIDN'T THINK THAT A *GIRL* MIGHT BE WORKING FOR BRANELESS, DID YOU? Y'ALL *SLEEP TIGHT,* NOW!

END PART ONE!

10

BART'S PUZZLE PAGE

THERE ARE 29 MISTAKES IN THIS PICTURE! CAN YOU FIND THEM ALL?

1. THERE IS NO MINUTE HAND ON THE CLOCK. 2. GROUNDSKEEPER WILLIE IS WEARING TWO DIFFERENT TYPES OF SHOES. 3. THE LETTER "s" IS REVERSED ON THE BLACKBOARD. 4. THE NUMBERS 8 AND 9 ARE REVERSED ON THE CLOCK. 5. MEXICO IS SHOWN NORTH OF THE UNITED STATES ON THE GLOBE. 6. THE REMAINING 24 MISTAKES ARE ON BART'S TEST PAPER, ALTHOUGH HE DOESN'T KNOW IT YET!

SOLVE THE MYSTERY
HELP PRINCIPAL SKINNER FIND OUT WHO SPRAYED GRAFFITI ON THE CHALK BOARD.

ANSWER: LISA! SHE'S THE ONLY STUDENT WHO KNOWS THAT "i" COMES BEFORE "e" EXCEPT AFTER "c."

CONNECT THE DOTS PUZZLE
WHAT DO YOU GET WHEN YOU CONNECT ALL THE DOTS?

ANSWER: A COMIC BOOK THAT'S NO LONGER IN MINT CONDITION, SUCKER!

WILD, WILD BART

PART II

WAKING UP, CAPTAIN SIMPSON?

WHERE AM I? WHERE'S *MARTIMUS*?

OH, YOUR PARTNER. I WOULDN'T WORRY ABOUT HIM. HE ESCAPED, BUT WE'LL FIND HIM. AS FOR WHERE YOU ARE...WELL...

...I'D SAY YOU'RE IN A BIT OF *TROUBLE*, WOULDN'T YOU?

JESSICA SAYS I'M NOT SUPPOSED TO TALK MUCH. MY NAME IS RALPH. I HAD FLAPJACKS FOR BREAKFAST. I HAVE A ROCK IN MY SHOE. ROCKS TASTE *BAD!*

SO YOU'RE LETTIN' A *GIRL* DO ALL YOUR TALKIN' FOR YA, HUH, BRANELESS?

JEEZ, LADY, YOUR BOYFRIEND SOUNDS LIKE A REAL *GENIUS!*

HE'S *NOT* MY BOYFRIEND!

HE MAY NOT MAKE MUCH SENSE WHEN HE TALKS, BUT HE INVENTED THIS *ELECTRICITY-PRODUCING MACHINE* FOR ME, AND IT'S GOING TO CHANGE *EVERYTHING!*

WITH *LIMITLESS* ELECTRICITY, WE'LL SOON HAVE *HAIR-DRYERS* AND *RADIOS* AND *COMPUTING MACHINES* AND *WHIRLPOOL BATHS* AND *TELEVISIONS!* AND WITH TELEVISIONS, WE'LL HAVE...

...ANIMATED CARTOONS!

13

LADY, YOU'RE JUST AS *CRAZY* AS YOUR *BOYFRIEND*.

HE'S *NOT* MY *BOYFRIEND*!

DADDY SAYS "SPURS SHOULD STAY ON YOUR *FEET!*"

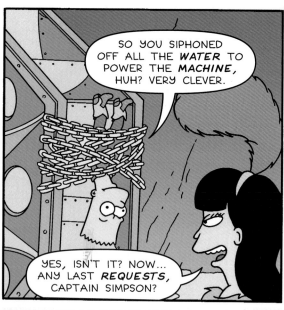

SO YOU SIPHONED OFF ALL THE *WATER* TO POWER THE *MACHINE*, HUH? VERY CLEVER.

YES, ISN'T IT? NOW... ANY LAST *REQUESTS*, CAPTAIN SIMPSON?

HERE'S MY CHANCE!

JUST ONE. GIVE ME BACK MY *HAT!*

OH, *THAT*. HERE YOU ARE...!

BUT YOU SAID I COULD BE A REAL *COWBOY!*

DID I FORGET TO MENTION THAT THE LAKE IS FILLED WITH *PIRANHA*?

ONCE NELSON PULLS THE LEVER TO START THE WATER WHEEL, YOU'LL GET TO MEET THEM *PERSONALLY!*

GOODBYE, CAPTAIN SIMPSON!

CHEW! TEAR! GNAW! SNAP! RIP! REND!

HA, HA!

RRRCHKT!

14

GUESS IT WASN'T SO SMART TO KEEP MY LOCK PICKS IN MY HAT.

FORTUNATELY, MARTIMUS *ALWAYS* PUTS SOMETHIN' USEFUL IN THE *HIDDEN COMPARTMENTS* IN MY BOOT!

TAP!

D'OH!

TAP! TAP!

A *BUBBLE WAND?* MARTIMUS IS REALLY *LOSING HIS EDGE,* MAN!

PLEASE BE SOMETHING *USEFUL* THIS TIME!

TAP! TAP! TAP!

ACID

AN *ACID-SHOOTING CANDY DISPENSER!* WAY TO GO, MARTIMUS!

A FEW MINUTES AND FOUR MELTED LOCKS LATER...

OWWWWWWW!!!

15

THEY AREN'T GOING TO GET AWAY WITH THIS. "TELEVISION"..."ANIMATED CARTOONS"...THEY'RE BOTH *NUTS!*

HEY, MARTIMUS! I KNEW IT WAS YOU IN *DISGUISE* ALL ALONG! THAT FACE IS TOO *UGLY* TO BE REAL!

WHY DIDN'T YOU *SAVE* ME?

BAAM!!!

OKAY, SO YOU'RE *NOT* MARTIMUS. ⸮GROAN!⸮

GET UP, HOMBRE, SO I CAN KNOCK YA *DOWN* AGAIN!

KEEP *LAUGHIN'*...

...SUCKER!!!

...HUH?

AAAAH!! THERE'S A *SHARK* IN MY BRITCHES! GET IT OUT! *GET IT OUT!!!*

THAT SOUNDS LIKE *NELSON'S* IN TROUBLE!

I JUST HAD AN IDEA FOR A VACUUM THAT CUTS HAIR!

GIVE IT UP, GIRLIE! YOU AND YOUR BOYFRIEND WILL *NEVER* ESCAPE!

HE'S *NOT MY BOYFRIEND!!!*

BAP!

WHEEEEE! I'M *FLYING*!

...OW, FLYING *HURTS*!

OW!

OW!

OW!!!

OH, WELL. I DON'T REALLY *NEED* BRANELESS ANYMORE, NOW THAT THE ELECTRICITY-MAKER IS FINISHED.

OH, YOU DON'T HAVE A HORSE, CAPTAIN? HOW *SAD!* GUESS I'LL JUST *ESCAPE* THEN! BYE, NOW!

NOT SO FAST, YOUNG LADY! MARTIMUS PRINCE, *MASTER* OF *DISGUISE,* AT YOUR SERVICE!

HE'S *NOT MY*...OH, NEVER MIND.

GOOD WORK, MARTIMUS! I GOT HER *BOYFRIEND* RIGHT HERE!

MY HEAD HAS MOUNTAINS!

SOON...

ANOTHER THREAT TO NATIONAL SECURITY DEFEATED, MARTIMUS, AND ALL THE *WATER* HAS BEEN RETURNED TO WHERE IT *BELONGS!*

YES. GOOD WORK, I SAY! "ANIMATED CARTOONS"...WHAT WAS THAT MADMAN *THINKING?*

I DON'T KNOW, BUT I'D SAY HE'S EASILY THE GREATEST *CRIMINAL GENIUS* THE WORLD HAS EVER KNOWN.

THAT DOGGIE HAS *HORNS!*

OH, *SHUT UP!*

THE LONESOME END!

WHEN WILL YOU *HOOLIGANS* LEARN THAT THE HALLS AND RECREATIONAL AREAS OF SPRINGFIELD ELEMENTARY ARE *MY* BEAT, AND ITS VERY INHABITANTS ARE *MINE* TO *SERVE* AND *PROTECT* FROM THE LIKES OF *YOU!*

TOO BAD YOU'RE MISSING A BADGE, A GUN, A NIGHTSTICK, OR ANYTHING ELSE THAT COULD *SCARE ME STRAIGHT!* HA, HA!

BE THAT AS IT MAY, I HAVE ARRANGED A *PERFECT PUNISHMENT* FOR YOU!

THE CASE OF THE HANGING SHOES

FROM THE SECRET FILES OF LISA SIMPSON

PRINCIPAL SKINNER, WHAT DID NELSON DO?

IT APPEARS YOUNG MUNTZ FELT THE URGE TO INFLICT A DEGREE OF *HUMILIATION* UPON A FELLOW STUDENT, BY THROWING *MARTIN PRINCE'S SHOES* OVER THE *POWER LINES*.

LISA, I KNOW I HAVE A CERTAIN REPUTATION TO UPHOLD, BUT *HONEST*, THIS TIME I *DIDN'T* DO IT.

FOR SOME *STRANGE REASON*, I BELIEVE YOU.

TERRY DELEGEANE
SCRIPT

IGOR BARANKO
PENCILS AND INKS

ART VILLANUEVA
COLORS

KAREN BATES
LETTERS

MATT GROENING
SUPER SLEUTH

SO HE WONTS ME TO FETCH THESE ORTHOPEDIC SHOES FROM THE WIRES, DOES HE? AH'D LIKE TO FETCH HIM A *FISTFUL OF WILLIE!*

...WOT'S THIS, NOW? SOMETHING IS *QUEER* IN THE STATE OF EDINBURGH.

WILLIE, WHAT'S TAKING SO LONG TO GATHER THE EVIDENCE?

SOMEONE'S USED SOME HIGH-FALUTIN' *ROPE TRICKERY* TO TIE THESE SHOES TOGETHER. I HAVEN'T BEEN WITNESS TO SUCH FINE KNOT WORK SINCE ME DAYS IN THE *SCOTTISH NAVY*.

WELL, CUT THE KNOT AND BRING IT HERE!

THAT'S IT!

SNAP!

?!

?!

A-HA! JUST AS I *SUSPECTED*. PRINCIPAL SKINNER, *LET NELSON GO!*

?!

20

NOW, LISA, GIVE ME BACK THAT KNOT THIS INSTANT!

BUT DON'T YOU SEE...

...THIS IS A *DUTCH CRINGLE* KNOT. IT IS A SPECIAL *KNOT* THAT'S USED TO FORM A HANDLE OR CONNECTION BETWEEN TWO POINTS OR OBJECTS.

ONLY THE *NIMBLEST* OF HANDS KNOWS HOW TO MAKE THIS KNOT AND HARDLY *ANYONE* IN SPRINGFIELD.

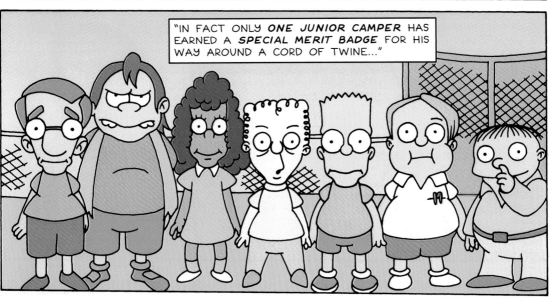

"IN FACT ONLY *ONE JUNIOR CAMPER* HAS EARNED A *SPECIAL MERIT BADGE* FOR HIS WAY AROUND A CORD OF TWINE..."

...MARTIN PRINCE!

LISA, THIS IS RIDICULOUS. CERTAINLY, YOU ARE NOT *ACCUSING* MARTIN PRINCE OF CONSTRUCTING AN *ELABORATE PLOT* TO FALSELY ACCUSE HIS WOULD BE *TORMENTOR*.

BUT IT'S *TRUE!* ALAS, I AM UNDONE. CHECK AND MATE, LISA. YOU MUST UNDERSTAND THAT MY ACTIONS WERE ONLY TO STAVE OFF MY FOE'S THREAT OF GIVING ME "*THE MOTHER OF ALL WEDGIES!*"

21

"AFTER BEING THREATENED WITHIN AN *INCH OF MY LIFE* BY NELSON, I DETERMINED TO *BEST HIM* AT HIS OWN GAME, TURNING THE PROVERBIAL TABLE ON MY ADVERSARY."

"I DEVISED A *SCHEME* TO SET-UP MY RIVAL FOR THE *FALL* OF HIS *YOUNG LIFE.*"

BUT THAT DOESN'T EXPLAIN HOW A *NOODLE-ARMED PANTY WAIST,* SUCH AS YOU, WITH NARY THE STRENGTH OF A *WEE BABE,* WAS ABLE TO HEFT THOSE SHOES OVER THE POWER LINES.

"THAT'S SIMPLE. I MERELY BORROWED THE *CATAPULT* FROM MY PRIZE-WINNING, EXTRA CREDIT DISPLAY OF *MEDIEVAL INSTRUMENTS OF WAR* AND CALCULATED THE PRECISE TRAJECTORY. THEN, I RETURNED IT IN A TRICE, AND NO ONE WAS THE WISER."

I THINK I HAVE HEARD ABOUT ENOUGH. OFF WITH THE *BOTH* OF YOU! YOU TOO, *BART!*

BUT *WAIT,* PRINCIPAL SKINNER! NELSON ONLY THREATENED MARTIN, AND BART DIDN'T DO ANY-THING AT ALL!

WHA-!

IT'S ALL A *MATTER OF TIME,* LISA, AND BESIDES, MOTHER'S GARDEN NEEDS TENDING. THOSE *HYDRANGEA BUSHES* WON'T JUST PRUNE THEMSELVES. AND THEN THERE'S THE WEEDING AND THE SEEDING...

≡SIGH≡

EH!

THE END

22

BART SIMPSON'S DAY OFF

WIGGLE PUPPY LIKES YOUR LEG.

≶SIGH≶

C'MON, BART. WHERE ARE YOU?

JAMES BATES–SCRIPT
CAROLYN KELLY–PENCILS
SCOTT MCRAE–INKS
LEE LOUGHRIDGE–COLORS
KAREN BATES–LETTERS
BILL MORRISON–EDITOR
MATT GROENING–GRAND MARSHALL

YIKES!

YANK!

WHAT'S THE BIG IDEA?

SHHH!

IN JUST A FEW MOMENTS THE BUS WILL COME AND GO, AND WE'LL BE *FREE!*

FREE?

SMELL THAT FRESH AIR! LOOK AT THE BLUE SKY! IT'S TOO NICE A DAY TO *WASTE* AT SCHOOL. TODAY IS A DAY FOR *FUN*.

FORGET IT, BART. WE'LL GET *CAUGHT*.

NO, WE WON'T.

BUT TODAY IS THE *SPRINGFIELD TOURNAMENT OF POSIES!* WE'LL BE WATCHING THE PARADE AT SCHOOL AND WON'T EVEN *HAVE* CLASSES.

SCHOOL IS SCHOOL. WITH EVERYONE PAYING ATTENTION TO THE *STUPID PARADE,* NO ONE WILL NOTICE WE'RE *MISSING*.

THE DAY IS *OURS!*

JUST LOOK AT THOSE POOR SAPS! C'MON, MILHOUSE...

...I *GUARANTEE* IT'LL BE FUN. SO WHAT'S IT GONNA BE? *SCHOOL OR FUN?*

I CHOOSE *FUN!*

LET THE *PARTY* BEGIN.

ARF!! ARF!!

SOON...

I DON'T KNOW, BART. IS SITTING OUTSIDE THE KWIK-E-MART **ALL** THE **FUN** YOU HAD IN MIND?

NO...

OKAY. WHAT'S NEXT?

...HOW ABOUT ...A *SQUISHEE RACE!*

READY? *GO!*

SSLLUUURRRPP!

...AND BART SIMPSON REMAINS THE *UNDEFEATED* AND *UNDISPUTED CHAMPION OF THE WORLD!*

MY BRAIN! MY POOR, *FROZEN BRAIN!*

PLEASE MOVE YOUR FRIEND OR PLACE HIM IN THE *TRASH RECEPTACLE* PROVIDED.

THANKS, BART.

AYE, CARUMBA!

STUDENT DISCIPLINE WEEKLY

"BEHIND THE WOODSHED" NOSTALGIA ISSUE

26

OUCH! WHAT'S THE BIG IDEA?

OH NO, WE'RE *SO* DEAD!

IT'S SUPERINTENDENT CHALMER'S *HENCHMAN*, LEOPOLD!

HELLO, MR. LEOPOLD, SIR. ARE YOU WORKING AS A *TRUANT OFFICER* TODAY?

OH, GOOD. MAY I ALSO INFORM YOU ABOUT THE TWO SCHOOL-AGED RAPSCALLIONS *HIDING* OUTSIDE?

YEAH, BUT I'M JUST HERE FOR A CLAMATO JUICE.

BEAKLOAF 3 for $1.

COME BACK HERE, YOU *LITTLE MAGGOTS!* YOU CAN TRY TO RUN AND YOU CAN TRY TO HIDE, BUT YOUR BUTTS ARE *MINE!*

IS *THIS* YOUR IDEA OF FUN, BART?

DID WE *LOSE* HIM?

VINTAGE CLOTHII

YANK!

27

EXCUSE ME. HAVE YOU SEEN TWO *WORTHLESS* LITTLE PUNKS RUNNING AROUND HERE?

AIN'T NO KIDS 'ROUND HERE, MAN.

UH, NO, WE DIDN'T SEE BART AND MILHOUSE.

HMM? OKAY. THANKS.

QUIET, YOU *NUMBSKULL!*

YOU ALMOST GOT US *CAUGHT*, MAN.

SORRY, I WAS *SCARED*.

JUST *RELAX* AND WE'LL GET OUT OF THIS.

BART, AM I *PRETTY*?

WHEN I FIND THOSE *TWERPS*, I'M GONNA TEAR 'EM A NEW PIE-HOLE.

OOF!

≋BURP!≋

WHUMP!

WHOA, *SONNY AND CHER!* MY HALLUCINATIONS ARE *IMPROVING*. I USUALLY SEE *THE CAPTAIN AND TENNILLE* AFTER I'VE BEEN TO MOE'S.

CAN YOU SEE THEM, TOO?

HE'S FIGURED IT OUT. WE'RE *BUSTED!*

NOT IF HE CAN'T *CATCH* US. *RUN!*

I KNEW YOU WERE TOO *ATTRACTIVE* TO BE CHER!

BART, HE'S GAINING, AND I'VE GOT A RUN IN MY *STOCKING.*

WE JUST NEED A BIG *DISTRACTION.* SOMETHING LIKE...

...THE PARADE!

SPRINGFIELD TOURNAMENT OF POSIES PARADE

29

HOLD ON. I THINK WE'VE FINALLY *LOST* HIM.

I DON'T THINK SO. *LOOK!*

YOU *WORMS* ARE ABOUT TO BE PUT ON THE *HOOK!*

BART, I'M *SCARED.*

ME TOO! *JUMP!*

OW-OW-OW.

OOF!

NOW *THOSE* ARE SOME BIG ELEPHANT PATTIES!

YOU'RE THE EXPERT.

GRAMPA!

HEY, WEREN'T YOU TWO ON *LAWRENCE WELK?*

IT'S *ME.* BART!

I *GOTCHA*, BOY!

OH NO, HERE GOES MY *NEW HIP*.

BOINK!

WHEW! I'M LUCKY THAT *MINI-CAR* RUNS ON TWO AAA BATTERIES.

I GOT YOU, ABE.

YOU'RE TOAST! YOUR SHENANIGANS END HERE!

NO WAY, JOSÉ. YOU GOT NOTHIN' ON US.

NOTHIN'?

LOOK WHERE WE ARE. WE'RE AT *SCHOOL*, DUDE!

YEAH!

WE LOVE POSIES!

WELL, MILHOUSE, I THINK WE'VE HELPED MY GRAMPA ENOUGH.

BEING THE MASONS' *OFFICIAL* POSIES PARADE SONNY AND CHER IMPERSONATORS HAS BEEN AN HONOR WE WON'T SOON FORGET.

HUH?

NICE *DRESS*, MILHOUSE.

THANKS, MRS. KRABAPPEL.

I CAN'T BELIEVE WE MADE IT!

JUST ANOTHER *VICTORY* FOR THE BOY, THE MYTH, THE LEGEND, THEY CALL...

...*BART SIMPSON!* LEOPOLD TELLS ME HE SPOTTED YOU TWO AT THE KWIK-E-MART, WHICH IS *NOT* ON THE PARADE ROUTE! *YOU'RE BUSTED!*

AW, MAN! WE'VE GOT A WHOLE MONTH IN *DETENTION!*

YEAH, I'M SORRY. I'M PRETTY USED TO IT, BUT IT'S GONNA BE *ROUGH* ON YOU!

DON'T BE SORRY. I'VE NEVER HAD SO MUCH *FUN*.

IN FACT, I HAD *SO* MUCH FUN THAT I'M *CUTTING* SCHOOL *TOMORROW!*

AH, MILHOUSE...

NO, DON'T TRY TO TALK ME OUT OF IT!

I DON'T HAVE THE HEART TO TELL HIM TOMORROW'S *SATURDAY!*

THE END

32

SIMPSONS COMICS PRESENTS

BART SIMPSON

☆ HIGH FLYER ☆

#6

US $2.50
CAN $3.50

WOO HOO!

HHOOOOOOOOOOOOOOOOOOOTTTTT!!!

PLINK!

RUSTLE! RUSTLE!

ERT! ERT!

OH, NO YOU DON'T, YOU *MANGY STRAY!*

YOU'RE NOT BRINGING YOUR *FILTHY GERMS* INTO *MY* BAR, YOU *DISGUSTING* STREET BEAST!

MY HAIR ITCHES.

IT'S PROBABLY JUST YOUR *HEAD LICE* KICKING IN AGAIN, BARNEY. C'MON, WE'LL CLEAN YOU UP BACK IN THE KITCHEN.

Toss!

?

:GULP!:

35

BLAM! BLAM! BLAM!

MOES TAVERN →

POLICE

SCREECH!

I LOVES SHOOTIN' THINGS! *ESPECIALLY* COPS!

AW, A KITTY!

A KITTY?! WHERE?

AIN'T IT *SWEET!* LIKE A SOOT-COVERED SNOWBALL.

LOOK OUT, KITTY!!

GEEZ, CHIEF, WHATEVER THOSE CROOKS HIT MUSTA BEEN *VAPORIZED.* THERE'S NOTHING HERE BUT A.....

DON'T LOOK NOW, BUT I THINK WE OWE THIS EASY CRIMINAL ROUNDUP TO...

BAAAHDOOOMMM

SCREEEECH!

The *Supercat* of Springfield!

CHRIS YAMBAR
STORY

DAN DECARLO
LAYOUTS

MIKE DECARLO
PENCILS/INKS

ART VILLANUEVA
COLORS

KAREN BATES
LETTERS

BILL MORRISON
EDITOR

MATT GROENING
SOMETHING FUNNY

THE HORROR!

DON'T MAKE ME WATCH! *ANYTHING* BUT THIS!

OH, PLEASE. IT'S JUST THE *NEWS!*

NEWS SNOOZE! POLITICS THIS. HUMAN INTEREST THAT! *BOOORING!*

BUT WITHOUT THE NEWS, HOW WE WOULD GET AN *UNBIASED PERSPECTIVE* ON FILTHY COMMIES, TREE-HUGGING ENVIRONMENTALISTS, AND GUN-LOVING, RIGHT-WING EXTREMIST REPUBLICANS?

GOOD POINT, DAD!

OH, BROTHER!

THE BOY RESPECTS HIS OLD DAD, AND THAT'S ALL I COULD EVER ASK...

SHHH! DUMMY UP, HOMER! CHECK OUT *THIS* NEWS STORY.

SPRINGFIELD POLICE GOT A *TIMELY ASSIST* IN STOPPING A CARLOAD OF CROOKS EARLIER THIS AFTERNOON BY NONE OTHER THAN WHAT IS NOW BEING CALLED... *THE SUPERCAT OF SPRINGFIELD*.

WITH US NOW IS POLICE CHIEF WIGGUM WITH AN *EYEWITNESS REPORT*. WHAT CAN YOU TELL US ABOUT THIS SIGHTING, CHIEF?

UH....WE WERE IN HOT PURSUIT OF THE *SHELBYVILLE THREE* WHEN THIS CAT JUMPED IN FRONT OF THEIR CAR AND STOPPED THEM COLD.

37

THEN, THE SUPERCAT *FLEW AWAY* LIKE SOME KIND OF BEAUTIFUL, STREAKY-BLACK SNOWBALL. HE...HE TURNED AND *WINKED* AT ME, TOO. IT WAS VERY *SPECIAL*.

COOL!

OOH, PLEASE! WHAT'S NEXT? FLYING HORSES? A SUPER-POWERED MONKEY?

MASKED DOGS WHO LIVE WITH THEIR BILLIONAIRE MASTERS IN GIANT CAVES FILLED WITH BATS???!!

ANIMALS ARE JUST *MINDLESS CREATURES* WHO EXIST TO SERVE AND ENTERTAIN US. THEY CAN'T BE OUR SUPERIORS. THEY CAN'T JUST...

...

EXCUSE ME, CHILDREN! I MUST *OVERFEED* CAT NOW!

MUST GO TO STORE AND BUY *FRESH HALIBUT FILLETS* AND *SWORDFISH STEAKS* NOW! WILL RETURN SOON...

....OH, YES! AND I WILL BRING BACK *COMIC BOOKS* FOR *BRILLIANT* SON, BART, AND COPIES OF "TEEN STEAM" FOR *WONDERFUL* DAUGHTER, LISA, TOO!

SNOWBALL II!! YOU...YOU'RE...

YES, BART. OUR LITTLE SNOWBALL II IS *REALLY*...THE SUPERCAT OF SPRINGFIELD! I DON'T KNOW HOW THIS ALL HAPPENED, BUT ONE THING IS FOR CERTAIN...

...WE'RE THE *LUCKIEST KIDS IN TOWN!*

YOU KNOW WHAT THIS MEANS, DON'T YOU, BART?

YEAH! SNOWBALL II CAN DO ALL MY HOMEWORK!

EVEN *BETTER* THAN THAT.

39

LOOK OUT, EVILDOERS! HERE WE COME!

WITH SNOWBALL II LEADING US AGAINST SPRINGFIELD'S CRIMINALS, WE CAN CLEAN THIS TOWN UP *FASTER* AND *BETTER* THAN *EVER!*

"ON MONDAY, THE SUPERCAT OF SPRINGFIELD AND HER *MYSTERIOUS SIDEKICKS* FOILED FAT TONY D'AMICO'S PLAN TO STEAL *SCRATCH-OFF LOTTERY TICKETS* AND REPLACE THEM WITH *SCRATCH AND SNIFFS!*"

"ON TUESDAY, THE SUPERCAT *REIGNITED* THE SPRINGFIELD TIRE YARD AFTER THE *PERPETUALLY-BURNING LANDMARK* WAS *EXTINGUISHED* BY *MEDDLING ECOLOGISTS* EARLIER IN THE WEEK."

"ON WEDNESDAY, THE SUPERCAT CONTRIBUTED ENTERTAINMENT TO THE INJURED DELIVERY PERSONS ASSOCIATION BY CHASING C. MONTGOMERY BURNS', USUALLY, BLOODTHIRSTY WATCHDOGS ALL OVER HIS ESTATE."

"ON THURSDAY, THE SUPERCAT GAVE *FREE X-RAYS* TO EVERY CITIZEN WHO VISITED THE KWIK-E-MART. OWNER APU NAHASAPEEMAPETILON WAS SO HAPPY WITH THE SALES FOR THE DAY, HE TOOK A *HALF-HOUR VACATION*. THERE WERE 63 *ARRESTS*."

"ON FRIDAY, THE ANDROIDS DUNGEON WAS SAVED FROM CLOSING WHEN SUPERCAT HELPED THE OWNER RAISE MONEY TO PAY HIS *UNPAID TAB* AT A NEARBY TACOMAT."

Meet the SUPERCAT of SPRINGFIELD autographs $25 each NO PETTING

CAN THINGS GET ANY *BETTER* FOR THE CITIZENS OF SPRINGFIELD NOW THAT THE AMAZING SUPERCAT IS HERE AMONG US? NINE OUT OF TEN CITIZENS SAY, NO!

THE REMAINING CITIZENS ARE IN JAIL. MORE TONIGHT AS THE *EXPLOITS* CONTINUE!

HMMMMMM!

WHAT A WEEK! I'M *BEAT*!

I KNOW WHAT YOU MEAN. WHO WOULD HAVE THOUGHT THAT BEING A CRIME FIGHTER COULD BE SO *TIRING*?! ⌐SIGH!⌐

AYE CARUMBA!

WELCOME, *DO-GOODERS!* WELCOME TO MY *SECRET HIDEOUT!* I HOPE THE *TRANSPORTER* BEAM DIDN'T DISTRESS YOU...

THUMP!

WHUMP!

...BUT THAT IS *MY JOB!!*

DR. COLOSSUS!!!

RELAX, CHILDREN. YOU'RE IN GOOD HANDS.

CLAP! CLAP!

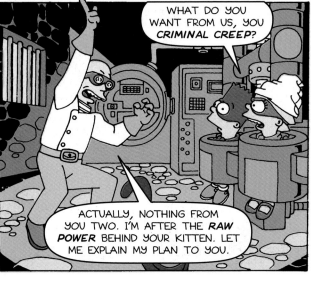

WHAT DO YOU WANT FROM US, YOU *CRIMINAL CREEP?*

ACTUALLY, NOTHING FROM YOU TWO. I'M AFTER THE *RAW POWER* BEHIND YOUR KITTEN. LET ME EXPLAIN MY PLAN TO YOU.

I'VE BEEN LOOKING FOR A *NEW POWER SOURCE* FOR A SPECIAL PROJECT OF MINE, AND THEN I SAW YOUR SUPERCAT'S *EXPLOITS* ON TV.

WHEN I REALIZED THE *POTENTIAL,* I TRANSPORTED YOU ALL HERE.

42

¡GASP!¡

WITH THE HELP OF OUR *LITTLE FRIEND* HERE, I'M GOING TO POWER MY CREATION AND LET IT LOOSE ON THE CITIZENS OF SPRINGFIELD UNTIL THERE'S NOTHING LEFT BUT A *GIANT SMOKING CRATER*.

THEN I'M GOING TO *TAKE OVER THE ENTIRE PLANET!*

AND JUST FOR THE RECORD, MY OUTFIT IS FIREPROOF, CONTAINS AN ANTI-FLIGHT GRAVITY FIELD, AND HAS ANTI-HYPNOTIC EYE SHIELDS.

DK 3000

SAY HELLO TO *DESTRUCTO-KAT 3000!*

SHUK!

I CAN'T GET LOOSE, LISA. I'M NOT STRONG ENOUGH.

WAIT A MINUTE, BART! *LOOK!*

BWA-HA-HA-HA!

WHAT IS GOING ON? YOU'RE NOT GOING TO...TO...

KLANG!

HAAACK!

HA! KNOCKED OUT BY A *SUPER HAIRBALL!*

SNOWBALL II! YOU DID IT! YOU *SAVED* SPRINGFIELD!

C'MON, LISA. LET'S GET OUTTA HERE AND LET THE COPS CLEAN UP THIS MESS!

I'M WITH YOU, BIG BROTHER. LET'S GO!

NOW, WHAT *IDIOT* WOULD GO AND LEAVE ONE OF THOSE *RADIOACTIVE THINGAMABOBS* LAYING AROUND LIKE THAT?!

I'LL BE BACK AGAIN, SPRINGFIELD, AND NEXT TIME I'LL *BRING YOU TO YOUR KNEES!*

SURE YOU WILL, FOUR EYES. SURE YOU WILL. IF *CHURCH* WON'T DO IT, THEN WHAT HOPE HAVE *YOU* GOT?

OHH! LOOKIT HOW CUTE YOU TWO LOOK DRESSED UP LIKE THEM *CRIME FIGHTERS* ON TV.

AND LOOKIT HERE. YOU EVEN DRESSED YOUR LITTLE CAT UP TO LOOK LIKE THE SUPERCAT OF SPRINGFIELD. HE'S SO CUTE I COULD JUST...

HAAACK!

OH, MY GAWWD! I'VE BEEN *BARFED* ON BY A COMMON *RAT CHASER*. OUTTA MY WAY! I'VE GOTTA SCRUB THIS FILTHY SPIT OFF MY FACE BEFORE I BECOME A *FREAK OF NATURE!!!*

TOO LATE!

THE END

45

AH, THERE'S NOTHIN' LIKE A HALF-FULL *TRASH DUMPSTER* TO SPICE UP A *BORING* WALK TO SCHOOL!

WHOEVER THOUGHT AN *EGGHEAD* LIKE *PROFESSOR FRINK* WOULD HAVE A BUNCH OF *COOL JUNK* LIKE *THIS?*

AND *THIS* IS JUST THE STUFF HE'S *THROWN OUT!*

UNH, I DON'T THINK WE SHOULD BE *MESSIN' AROUND* BACK HERE, BART! THOSE *CHEMICALS* LOOK KINDA *DANGEROUS!*

DO NOT PLAY ON OR AROUND
THANK YOU, FRINK LABORATORIES

BART SIMPSON AND **MILHOUSE VAN HOUTEN** IN:

"THE INVISIBLE NERD!"

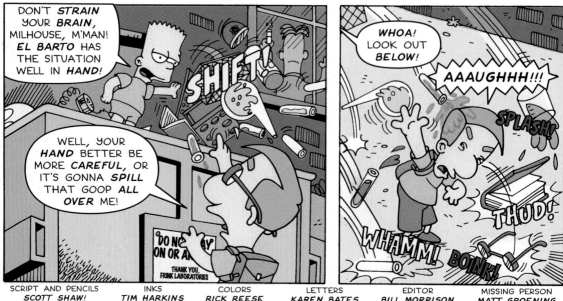

DON'T *STRAIN* YOUR *BRAIN,* MILHOUSE, M'MAN! *EL BARTO* HAS THE SITUATION WELL IN *HAND!*

WELL, YOUR *HAND* BETTER BE MORE *CAREFUL,* OR IT'S GONNA *SPILL* THAT GOOP *ALL OVER* ME!

SHIFT!

DO NOT PLAY ON OR AROUND
THANK YOU, FRINK LABORATORIES

WHOA! LOOK OUT *BELOW!*

AAAUGHHH!!!

SPLASH!

THUD!

WHAMM!

BOINK!

SCRIPT AND PENCILS **SCOTT SHAW!**   INKS **TIM HARKINS**   COLORS **RICK REESE**   LETTERS **KAREN BATES**   EDITOR **BILL MORRISON**   MISSING PERSON **MATT GROENING**

I'VE BEEN *HIT!* I'M A *GONER!* MY ENTIRE SHORT *LIFE* SHOULD START FLASHING BEFORE MY EYES ANY MINUTE NOW!

DO NOT PLAY ON OR AROUND

THANK YOU, FRINK LABORATORIES

BUT I CAN'T *SEE!* YOU *BLINDED* ME WITH THAT STUFF, BART! BECAUSE OF *YOU,* I'M GONNA *MISS* MY OWN PRE-DEATH *FLASHBACKS!*

HMM, THIS IS THE *PERFECT OPPORTUNITY* TO *LIVEN UP* A BORING DAY...*AND* HAVE A LITTLE *FUN* AT OL' MILHOUSE'S *EXPENSE,* TOO!

AH, *THERE* THEY ARE--JUST WHAT I WAS *LOOKING* FOR!

I'LL *POCKET* THESE *EYEGLASSES* THAT MILHOUSE DROPPED!

HAH! CHILDREN CAN BE SO *CRUEL!* AND I JUST HAPPEN TO BE AN *OVERACHIEVER* IN *CHILDISH CRUELTY!*

DON'T WORRY, MILHOUSE, OL' BUDDY, I'M *HERE!*

BUT UNHH-- MILHOUSE, WH-WHERE ARE *YOU?*

I'M RIGHT *HERE,* BART! OR DID THAT STUFF MAKE *YOU* BLIND, *TOO?*

47

WAIT A MINUTE... YOU *CAN'T* SEE ME? B-BUT THEN, *THAT* WOULD MEAN--!

THAT'S *RIGHT,* MILHOUSE! PROFESSOR FRINK'S CHEMICALS MUST HAVE *TRANSFORMED* YOU TO BECOME (DARE I EVEN *SAY* IT?)--

PSST, I'M OVER *HERE,* BART!

--*INVISIBLE* TO THE *HUMAN EYEBALL!!!*

REALLY? YOU *THINK* SO?

NAHHH, IT *CAN'T* BE...

LOOK, MILHOUSE, AS ANY SELF-RESPECTING *COMIC BOOK FAN* KNOWS, *DAREDEVIL* GAINED HIS SENSORY *SUPER-POWERS* WHEN *A RADIOACTIVE ISOTOPE ACCIDENTALLY BLINDED HIM!*

NOW DO YOU BELIEVE THAT I REALLY, TRULY, *CAN'T* SEE YOU, MILHOUSE?

UH, I GUESS *THAT* MAKES SENSE, SINCE *I* CAN'T SEE ME, *EITHER*...BART, YOU'RE *RIGHT*--I CAN'T SEE A *THING!!!*

GOOD LORD! ⋶CHOKE!⋶ THERE'S NO OTHER EXPLANATION --I *AM* INVISIBLE*!!!*

48

WELL, NOW THAT WE'VE ESTABLISHED *THAT*, ARE YOU READY TO *REAP* THE *BENEFITS* OF YOUR NEW-FOUND *INVISIBILITY*?

OH, THIS IS GONNA BE SO *SWEET*...

WHOA, YOU *BET*!

DO NOT PLAY ON OR AROUND

THANK YOU, FRINK LABORATORIES

UH, IT JUST *OCCURRED* TO ME, BART...IF I'M *BLIND*, JUST HOW AM I GONNA *SEE* THOSE "BENEFITS" YOU MENTIONED?

JUST *STICK* WITH *ME*, MILHOUSE! I'LL BE HAPPY TO PROVIDE A PLAY-BY-PLAY *NARRATION* DESCRIBING THE HILARIOUS *HIJINKS* THAT ARE *BOUND* TO *ENSUE*!

"HILARIOUS HIJINKS"? MAN, I SPEND *WAY* TOO MUCH *TIME* READING THE *PROGRAM DESCRIPTIONS* IN *TV GUIDE*.

THANKS, BART! YOU'RE A REAL *PAL*!

DON'T *SWEAT* IT, AMIGO! OUR *FIRST* SCHEDULED STOP WILL BE--

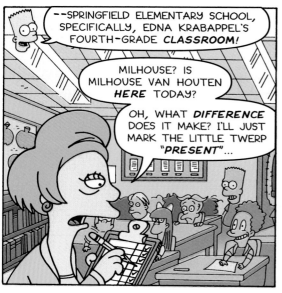

--SPRINGFIELD ELEMENTARY SCHOOL, SPECIFICALLY, EDNA KRABAPPEL'S FOURTH-GRADE *CLASSROOM!*

MILHOUSE? IS MILHOUSE VAN HOUTEN *HERE* TODAY?

OH, WHAT *DIFFERENCE* DOES IT MAKE? I'LL JUST MARK THE LITTLE TWERP *"PRESENT"*...

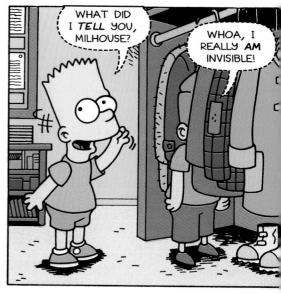

WHAT DID I *TELL* YOU, MILHOUSE?

WHOA, I REALLY *AM* INVISIBLE!

NEXT, THE SPRINGFIELD ELEMENTARY SCHOOL CAFETERIA, A PLACE JUST BEGGING FOR YOUR MISCHIEVOUS TOUCH, O INVISIBLE ONE!

WATCH ME *FREAK OUT* LUNCH LADY DORIS.

I AM THE *GHOST* OF ALL THE MYSTERY *MEAT* YOU SERVED LAST SEMESTER! YOU WILL BE *PUNISHED* FOR YOUR *CRIMES!*

HEY, CAN WE GET A *MOP* OVER HERE?

LOOK OUT, MILHOUSE, YOU *KNOW* THIS CAFETERIA HAS A STRICT *"NO TIPPING"* POLICY!

SPLORK!

WOW, SHE WAS SO *SCARED,* SHE *ALMOST DROPPED* HER *SERVING-SCOOP!*

PROFESSOR VON SIMPSON'S *HYGIENE CLASS* IS NOW IN SESSION!

GREETINGS, LADIES! IT IS *I,* THE INVISIBLE *PHANTOM* OF THE *LAVATORY!* ϶BWOOOHAHAHAH!!!϶

EEEEEEEEEEEEEEE!!!

ARGHH! LOOK OUT! YOU'RE *TRAMPLING* ME!

YOU MAY BE *INVISIBLE,* MILHOUSE, BUT YOU SURE AIN'T *INVULNERABLE!*

STAMPEDE!

50

WHAT SAY WE TAKE A TRIP TO THE *ANDROID'S DUNGEON* FOR SOME "FREE" READING...

PSST, MILHOUSE, HOW ABOUT TAKING THAT BOX OF OLD *COMICS!* WE CAN READ 'EM AND BRING 'EM BACK, AND NO ONE WILL KNOW!

UH, I *DUNNO*, BART...ISN'T THAT KINDA LIKE *STEALING?*

TELL YOUR FRIEND THAT I *APPRECIATE* HIM HAULING AWAY THOSE OLD COMICS! THEIR *LAST* OWNER HAD THE *CHICKEN POX*, AND NOW THEY'RE TOO *INFECTIOUS* TO SELL TO ANYONE!

:PANT!: :WHEEZE!: :PUFF!:

RICHIE

YEAH, I'LL GIVE HIM THE WORD... ...*EVENTUALLY!*

A BOY NEEDS TO BE *NURTURED*, EVEN AN *INVISIBLE* BOY! AND WHAT COULD BE MORE *NURTURING* THAN YOUR VERY OWN HOME-SWEET-*HOME?*

AND SO THEN I TOLD THAT GOOD-FOR NOTHING, DEAD-BEAT DAD, EX-HUSBAND OF MINE...

UH, MOM? HI, MOM! I BET YOU'RE WONDERING WHY YOU CAN'T *SEE* ME, HUH, MOM? MOM? *MOMMY?!?*

MILHOUSE, DOES YOUR MOM HAVE "*CALL-WAITING*" ON HER PHONE?

UH, YEAH, I *THINK* SO!

MAYBE YOU SHOULD JUST *CALL* HER ON THAT *CELL PHONE* AN' TELL HER YOU'RE INVISIBLE?!

NO, SHE *NEVER* ACCEPTS MY CALLS...

AND *FINALLY*, WE ASK THE QUESTION: WHAT'S A *DAY* WITHOUT A BIT OF MULTICULTURAL *NIGHTLIFE?*

I URGE YOU, PLEASE, KEEP YOUR *HANDS* WITHIN *VIEW* AT ALL TIMES, YOU MERRY YOUNG *TRICKSTER!*

NO *PROBLEMO*, APU! I'M AS *INNOCENT* AS THE DRIVEN *SNOW CONES!*

GRGLGRGLGRGLLLL

SPEAKING OF WHICH... AIEEEE!

LEASE
GIVE
GUIL
BUTZ STIX!
GIVE

COME BACK HERE, YOU YOUNG *RUFFIANS!* I'LL GIVE YOU A *FREE TASTE*--OF MY STRAIGHT-FROM-THE-SPIGOT *JAIPOORIAN JUSTICE!*

I DON'T *GET* IT, BART! YOU SAID I'D BE ABLE TO DRINK ALL THE MANGO-CHUTNEY *SQUISHEES* I COULD HOLD, BUT *APU* BUSTED ME RED-HANDED!

UH, *SORRY*, MILHOUSE! I GUESS YOUR *INVISIBILITY* CAN BE TEMPORARILY *CANCELLED OUT* BY A MASSIVE "*BRAIN-FREEZE*"!

51

THE NEXT DAY...

WHAT'S WITH THE WACKY GET-UP, O *INVISIBLE* ONE?

WHEN SPRINGFIELD'S CITIZENRY SEES THIS *STUFF* MYSTERIOUSLY *FLOATING* IN *MID-AIR*, THEY'LL GO *NUTSOID*! IT'LL BE *BIG LAUGHS*, BART!

MILHOUSE, DO YOU HAVE MY *FUR COAT*? IT'S GENUINE "*CUBIC MINKONIUM*"!

OH, WE'RE GONNA GET SOME BIG *LAUGHS*, ALL RIGHT!

SUCKER!

BEFORE LONG...

OH, *NO*, LOOK WHO'S COMING *THIS WAY*!

UH, THAT'S REAL EASY FOR *YOU* TO SAY, BART...

=GRUMBLE= =MUMBLE!=

=SNORT!=

IT'S *JIMBO*, *DOLPH* AND *KEARNEY*!

=GRUNT!=

OBOY! *BULLIES AHOY!*

=SNUK!=

IT'S *PAYBACK TIME* FOR THE "*INVISIBLE AVENGER*"! HEY, *DUDES!* AM I *BLOWING* YOUR *MINDS* YET?

HONK!

HOOOOOOONNK!

I WAS *AFRAID* THIS MIGHT HAPPEN...

52

WHAT'S WITH *FOUR-EYES* HERE?

MAYBE HE'S BEEN GUZZLING TOO MANY *BUZZ COLAS*?

WHATEVER THE REASON, I THINK WE OUGHTA *POUND* THIS WEIRDO...

...JUST ON *GENERAL PRINCIPLES*, Y'KNOW?

HONK!

HOOOOOONNK!

MEANWHILE, *BART'S* EXPERIENCING A SURPRISING *CRISIS-OF-CONSCIENCE*...

SO, WHAT SHOULD I *DO*, GUYS?

POOF!

POOF!

BART, *STEP IN* BEFORE THOSE HOODS MAKE *LUNCHMEAT* OUT OF MILHOUSE!

BART, BEAT YER FEET OUTTA HERE AND *SAVE* YOUR *OWN* YELLOW HIDE, CHUM!

C'MON, YOU CUTE LI'L CARTOON *CLICHÉS*, I NEED A STRAIGHT ANSWER--

--NOW!

53

WELL, SO MUCH FOR MY BEING *REASONABLE*. IT'S TIME TO USE THE *DIRECT* APPROACH!

HIII YAHHH!

PLUCK!

SHUUUNNK!

ARGHH!!!! I'M *HIT*!

SOMEHOW IT *FIGURES* THAT *MY CONSCIENCE* WOULD HAVE SUCH EXTREME *MOOD-SWINGS*!

THWUMP!

I HOPE YOU'VE RETURNED ALL YOUR *LIBRARY BOOKS* ON TIME, YOU LITTLE *MOLE RAT*!

YEAH, 'CAUSE YOU WON'T BE *LEAVIN'* YOUR *HOSPITAL BED* ANY TIME SOON!

WELL, I'M PRETTY SURE THAT *ONE* OF US IS, AND IT AIN'T *ME*!

EXCUSE ME, GUYS, BUT I DON'T THINK YOU *REALLY* WANT TO *CLOBBER* MY FRIEND HERE!

THEN AGAIN, MAYBE I'M *NOT* INVISIBLE, AND YOU'RE JUST *LOSING* YOUR *MINDS*!?!

SKIDDD!!!

WE *DON'T*? WHY TH' HECK *NOT*?

WELL, HE'S *INVISIBLE*.

HE *AIN'T* INVISIBLE!

SURE HE IS. I'LL *PROVE* IT!

OKAY, DUDE, *PROVE* IT *NOW*!

WELLLLL, LOOK AT IT *THIS* WAY...

...YOU *CAN'T* SEE GAS, BUT IT *CAN POISON* YOU, RIGHT?

YOU *CAN'T* SEE *RADIATION*, BUT IT CAN BURN YOU, RIGHT?

YOU *CAN'T* SEE *GERMS*, BUT THEY *CAN* MAKE YOU *SICK*, RIGHT?

WELL, IF SOMETHING *INVISIBLE* THAT YOU *CAN'T* SEE CAN DO ALL *THAT* TO YOU... ...JUST *IMAGINE* WHAT SOMETHING *INVISIBLE* THAT YOU *CAN* SEE *WILL* DO TO YOU!

LET'S GET *OUTTA* HERE!* HE'S USIN' *CONTRADICTORY LOGIC!*

SO *WHY* ARE WE *RUNNIN'*? THAT *INVISIBILITY* ACT OF HIS AIN'T *CONVINCING!*

WHO *CARES*, DUDE? HE SURE *CONVINCED* ME HE'S *DANGEROUS* AS ALL GET-OUT!!!

WELL, I GUESS THE "INVISIBLE AVENGER" SHOWED *THEM!*

ːPHEW!ː

*MANDATORY "BAD GUY" DIALOGUE

HEY, I CAN *SEE* AGAIN! AND I CAN SEE *MYSELF* AGAIN, TOO!

YEAH, *PROFESSOR FRINK'S* CHEMICAL *FORMULA* MUST'VE FINALLY *WORN OFF!*

ːWAKKA-DING-*HOY*!ː DID SOMEONE MENTION *MY* NAME?

YOU BOYS WILL HAVE TO *EXCUSE* ME, BUT I'M *LATE* FOR MY *WATER-SKIING* LESSON! ːVOIVEL!ː

AY-YI-YIKES!!

AHOOOGAHHH!

THE END!

55

"24 HOURS IN THE LIFE OF RALPH WIGGUM!"

6:14 AM

SPRINGFIELD

OHHH, WHAT A *NIGHTMARE!*

6:29 AM

MMM...THIS NEW *TOOTHPASTE* IS *SCRUMPDIDDLEY-UMPTIOUS!*

BRUSHA BRUSHA BRUSHA

ARRR, IT BE *AWFUL* FISHY!

FRYIN' DUTCHMAN BRAND **ANCHOVY PASTE**

6:54 AM

OOPSIE! I FEEL A *BREEZE* ON MY *BUM-BUM!*

7:15 AM

Y'KNOW, I NEVER REALLY *"GET"* THIS COMIC STRIP, BUT THERE'S SOMETHING KINDA *FAMILIAR* ABOUT THIS *'ZIPPY THE PINHEAD'* FELLA...

I WOULDN'T BE *EATING* THOSE DONUTS IF I WERE YOU, SWEETHEART...

LOOK, DADDY, *"OFFICER PUPPY"* LIKES *DONUTS* TOO! MMM... *CHOCOLATEY!*

7:33 AM

SEARCH AN' SEIZE TH' DAY, LI'L CITIZEN!

MY DADDY TELLS ME THAT SAME THING *EVERY DAY*...

...SOMEDAY, I'M GONNA ASK HIM JUST WHAT IT *MEANS!*

SCRIPT AND PENCIL ART BY SCOTT SHAW!   INKED BY SCOTT MCRAE   COLORED BY RICK REESE   LETTERED BY KAREN BATES   EDITED BY BILL MORRISON   ENCOURAGED BY MATT GROENING

"RALPH WIGGUM" CREATED BY CLANCY AND SARA WIGGUM

7:37 AM

OOH... *SHINY!*

7:49 AM

WHEEE! I'M A *FLYING SAUCER!* ZOOM!

MR. KITTY-CAT, TAKE ME TO YOUR *LEADER--* GARFIELD!

8:02 AM

HEY, *I* LIKE TO *DIG*, TOO!

YEAH, KID, I CAN *SEE* THAT! NOW WOULD YOU *STOP* DIGGIN'? *PLEASE?*

PICK!

PICK!

ECHHH...

8:14 AM

SUPERFLY GLUE-WORKS
"WE REALLY STICK IT TO THE MAN"

ⵣSNIFF!ⵣ
ⵣSNIFF!ⵣ

MMMM...IT SMELLS *NICE*, LIKE OLD *HORSIES!*

8:23 AM

COMING SOON
THE REVENGE OF THE MONSTER THAT DEVOURED SHEL...IN EXT... SATISFY...

CIRC' DE PRETENTIO
FEATURING A VERY SPECIAL GREASEPAINT TRIBUTE TO JERRY LEWIS

BOY-OH-BOY! in concert!
47 DIFFERENT BOY BANDS!!!
NOYZ FROM BOYZ & ARMZ 2 HOLD-U, TWEEN TOWN CHEF BOY-R-DEE! --AND MANY MORE!!!

...ASAURUS IS BACK!!!

POST NO BILLS

SPRINGFIELD SPORTS ARENA!!!
FOR CUT... DON'T MISS THE RED SLUSH TOUR OF ITCHY AND SCRATCHY ON ICE!!

RIDE CHUNK-BLOWR...!!!
NOW AT SPRINGFIELD'S NEWEST THEME PARK, WHIPLASH ACRES

NEAT-O KEEN-O!

BUT *MY* NAME'S NOT "BILL"...

8:30 AM

HI, LISA! OFFICER PUPPY AND I HAD *DONUTS* FOR BREAKFAST!

UH, DON'T LOOK *NOW*, RALPH...

...BUT I THINK YOU'VE STILL *GOT* A BIG ONE AROUND YOUR *NECK!*

BRRRRRRINNNNGGGG!!!

57

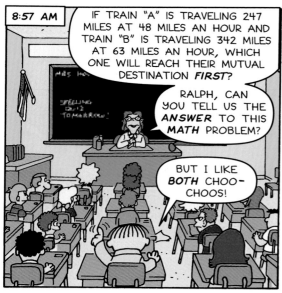

8:57 AM

IF TRAIN "A" IS TRAVELING 247 MILES AT 48 MILES AN HOUR AND TRAIN "B" IS TRAVELING 342 MILES AT 63 MILES AN HOUR, WHICH ONE WILL REACH THEIR MUTUAL DESTINATION *FIRST*?

RALPH, CAN YOU TELL US THE *ANSWER* TO THIS *MATH* PROBLEM?

BUT I LIKE *BOTH* CHOO-CHOOS!

9:32 AM

CLASS, CAN EACH OF YOU FIND WHERE YOU *LIVE*?

:SIGH!: VERY *ACCURATE*, RALPH.

CITY OF SPRINGFIELD

EARTH'S MOON

10:43 AM

OOH, *GOODY*! I GET TO PLAY *CENTER* POSITION!

BUT ISN'T *DODGE-BALL* PLAYED WITH ONLY *ONE* BALL?

11:22 AM

MISS HOOVER, IS THIS A *GOOD* GRADE OR A *BAD* GRADE?

:SIGH!: RALPH, *YOUR* GUESS IS AS GOOD AS *MINE*.

12:47 PM

OOH, WHO WANTS TO *TRADE* LUNCHES?

LET'S SEE, *I'VE* GOT A BOLOGNA SANDWICH, A BAG OF CORN CHIPS, AND AN APPLE!

WELL, *I'VE* GOT A TUNA FISH SAND-WICH, CELERY STICKS WITH PEANUT BUTTER, AND A BANANA!

NUMMY-NUMS! *I'VE* GOT A JAR OF *PASTE*!

2:31 PM

WOW, JUST *LISTEN* TO RALPH *SNORE*!

ZZZZZZZZ

YEAH, HE'S REALLY *SAWING LOGS*!

58

3:05 PM

BRRrrrRINNNNGGGG!!!

MY *BRAIN* HURTS!

3:12 PM

THIS DOGGIE WAS MY *FAVORITE* CARTOON CHARACTER!

?

JIGGA JIGGA JIGGA JIGGA

RIDE POOCHIE!

BUT HE *DIED* ON THE WAY BACK TO HIS HOME *PLANET!*

3:28 PM

THANKS, KID, BUT I REALLY *DON'T* NEED ANY *HELP!* NOW HURRY ALONG! I'VE *GOTTA* GET THIS THING *FINISHED* BY *TONIGHT,* OR ELSE THE CLIENT'S GONNA KICK MY *BUHHH---*?!?

MISTER, I *PAINT* WHAT I *SEE!*

SLAP! SLAP!

SPRINGFIELD SAVINGS

4:07 PM

AND TO THINK THAT I SAW IT ON... HEY, WHAT STREET *IS* THIS, ANYWAY?

MULBERRY STREET

4:19 PM

LITTERS O' CRITTERS
PET SHOP

HI, MISTER, I'M JUST VISITING *GOLDIE!* HE'S THE ONE WHO LOOKS LIKE *FONZIE,* ONLY *TALLER!*

4:31 PM

DINGDINGDING! CLANG!

SPRINGFIELD VIDEO ARCADE

BLEEP! DOINK! BLOOP!

VROOP!

:GIGGLE!:

THIS IS THE *BESTEST* VIDEO GAME *EVER!*

TRICKLE!

59

4:46 PM

DO *I* LIVE HERE? IF I *DON'T*, THAT DOGGIE LOOKS *AWFULLY* FAMILIAR!

⦂GROAN!⦂

LARD LAD DONUTS

5:53 PM

⦂SIGH!⦂

GOLDIE FUND

SPRINKLE!

FISH FOOD

6:15 PM

GOSH, HOMEWORK IS *HARD!* EVEN *HARDER* THAN REMEMBERING TO *BREATHE!*

6:57 PM

SO, HONEY, WHAT HAPPENED TO *YOU* TODAY?

OH, NOTHIN' *SPECIAL,* MOMMY...

GOOD...*PASS* ME THEM *PORK CHOPS,* WILL YA?

7:22 PM

AND *NOW*, BACK TO OUR REGULAR PROGRAMMING HERE ON THE *CAR-CHASE NETWORK*...

DADDY, CAN'T WE WATCH THE *CARTOON CHANNEL* FOR A WHILE?

NAHH, THOSE *"ROADRUNNER" CARTOONS* ALWAYS *DEPRESS* ME! THEY'VE GOT LOTSA *PURSUITS,* BUT THAT *GOOD-GUY COYOTE* ALWAYS GETS *CLOBBERED!* Y'KNOW, I REALLY *HATE* THAT STINKIN' BIRD!

8:24 PM

LOOK, DUCKIE, I'M *SHRIVELING* INTO A BIG OL' *PRUNE!*

UH-OH! I HOPE DADDY DOESN'T PUT ME IN A *DANISH PASTRY!*

SPLISH! SPLASH!

8:42 PM

OOOH, I ALWAYS FORGET. *WHICH* HOLE DOES MY *HEAD* GO THROUGH?

8:53 PM

WELL, *SWEET DREAMS* MY LITTLE CITIZEN! DON'T LET THE *BEDBUGS* BITE!

SMEK!

OH, THESE *AREN'T* BEDBUG BITES, DADDY! *THESE* BITES ARE FROM *DEER TICKS!*

9:06 PM

CLAP *ON*, CLAP *OFF*, CLAP ON, CLAP OFF--

CLAP! CLAP!

9:07 PM

PLOP!

CLICK!

ZZZZZZZZ

⧙WHIMPER!⧘...MAKE IT...⧙MUMBLE⧘...STOP... ⧙WHIMPER!⧘

6:14 AM

SPRINGFIELD

OHHH, WHAT A *NIGHTMARE!*

NEVER *THE END!*

61

SIMPSONS COMICS PRESENTS

BART SIMPSON
BOY OF MYSTERY

#7

US $2.50
CAN $3.50

Free Donuts

See You Later, ALLIGATOR!

THREE MONTHS FROM NOW WE WILL BE HAVING OUR *ANNUAL SCIENCE FAIR* HERE AT SPRINGFIELD ELEMENTARY SCHOOL, AND WE ARE EXPECTING EACH OF YOU TO *PARTICIPATE* BY CREATING YOUR OWN *UNIQUE EXPERIMENT*.

SCIENCE BITES!

COME ON, BART! EVERYTHING AROUND US IS THE RESULT OF SOME FORM OF SCIENCE.

OKAY, EXCEPT FOR THE *FRANKEN-STEIN MONSTER, MONKEYS IN SPACE,* AND *TV,* SCIENCE HAS BEEN ONE BIG *LETDOWN.* SHOW ME ONE *OTHER* REASON WHY I SHOULD GIVE UP MY *VALUABLE TIME* FOR SOME DUMB SCIENCE FAIR.

SHHHHHH!

CHRIS YAMBAR STORY	**DAN DECARLO** LAYOUTS	**LUIS ESCOBAR** PENCILS
MIKE ROTE INKS	**RICK REESE** COLORS	**KAREN BATES** LETTERS
	MATT GROENING SEWER INSPECTOR	

THE **SPONSOR** OF THIS YEAR'S FAIR IS THE OWNER OF *THE ANDROIDS DUNGEON*, WHO WOULD LIKE TO EXPLAIN...

SILENCE, EARTHLING! ALLOW ME TO INSTRUCT THE **MICRO-MINIONS** SEATED BEFORE US!

OOOF!

WHUMP!

HARKEN TO MY WORDS, CHILDREN OF THE ATOM! *THREE* OF YOU WILL BE **REWARDED** FOR YOUR EFFORTS TO *EXALT* SCIENCE THROUGH **EXPERIMENTATION!**

THE REST OF YOU WILL FEEL THE *VICIOUS STING OF FAILURE* AND CARRY IT ON INTO ADULT LIFE.

BEFORE THERE WAS A **PRIMORDIAL OOZE** FOR YOU TO CLIMB OUT OF--THERE WAS **SCIENCE!** BEFORE THE FIRST ROMULAN EVER APPEARED ON NETWORK TELEVISION--THERE WAS **SCIENCE!** BEFORE THE FIRST SQUISHEE WAS EVER DISPENSED AND SOLD WITH A MICROWAVED BURRITO--THERE WAS **SCIENCE!**

VERILY, IT WAS SCIENCE THAT GAVE US THE HOLOGRAPHIC TRADING CARD, THE BASIS FOR SCIENCE FICTION STORIES, AND THE DEEP DISH PIZZA...AND VERILY I SAY THAT IT WILL BE **YOUR** SCIENTIFIC EXPERIMENT WHICH WILL DETERMINE WHETHER OR NOT YOU WILL WIN ONE OF THREE **SHOPPING SPREES** AT THE ANDROIDS DUNGEON VALUED AT **$25 EACH!**

YOU ARE DISMISSED. GO TO YOUR BUSES, CHILDREN. PLEASE WALK, DON'T--

RUN! ARISE, FOR YOUR ESCAPE PODS HAVE ARRIVED! IT IS TIME TO RETURN TO YOUR NATIVE HOMEWORLDS! GO! FLEE!

THAT MAN IS A RAVING LUNATIC! WHO IN THEIR RIGHT MIND WOULD LISTEN TO SUCH...

...INSANITY?

AND NOW, I TAKE MY LEAVE TO EXPLORE NEW HORIZONS AT THE NEIGHBORING TACO MAT. GOOD DAY, SIR.

ONE WEEK LATER...

...NOW, IF I CAN ONLY ISOLATE THE PROPER...

GLAH WOOOSHA!

GAH! I CAN'T EVEN *THINK* WITH ALL THIS NOISE!

GLAH WOOOSHA!

CAN'T YOU GO SOMEWHERE ELSE? I'M TRYING TO...

GLAH WOOOSHA!

WHAT IN THE WORLD ARE YOU *DOING*, BART?!?

I'M FLUSHING BABY ALLIGATORS DOWN THE TOILET. WHAT ARE *YOU* DOING?

DANGER: CONTAINS BABY ALLIGATORS

66

GOODBYE #52. MAKE ME *PROUD*.

I'M TELLING MOM!

DANGER: CONTAINS BABY ALLIGATORS

GLAH WOOOSHA!

RELAX, LISA. REMEMBER WHEN WE GOT MONEY FROM DAD FOR OUR SCIENCE PROJECTS? YOU WENT OUT AND BOUGHT *YOUR* STUFF AT NERDS 'R' US, AND I WENT TO THE *PET SHOP*!

WHAT DO YOU MEAN? I DON'T SEE ANY *SCIENCE PROJECT*!

THAT'S THE *BEAUTY* OF IT, LIS. IT'S A SCIENCE PROJECT THAT DOES ITS *OWN* WORK. PLUS, NOBODY CAN *COPY* IT. MY EXPERIMENT IS COMPLETELY SAFE FROM PRYING EYES.

I'M A *CINCH* TO WIN *FIRST PRIZE*!

I'M AFRAID I DON'T UNDERSTAND.

WELCOME TO MY *SECRET LABORATORY*! THIS IS WHERE I AM DEFYING THE *LAWS OF NATURE* TO CREATE A *NEW LIFE FORM*! RIGHT UNDER THE *UNSUSPECTING FEET* OF THE PEOPLE OF SPRINGFIELD.

AND I OWE IT ALL TO DAD'S BOSS.

MR. *BURNS*?!

67

REMEMBER WHEN WE CAUGHT THAT *THREE-EYED MUTANT FISH*? MR. BURNS *CREATED* THAT FISH WHEN HE DUMPED *RADIOACTIVE WASTE* INTO OUR RIVER.

PEOPLE WERE SURE MAD ABOUT THAT.

SO WHY DO YOU THINK HE *REBUILT* THE ENTIRE *SEWAGE SYSTEM* FOR SPRINGFIELD?

SO WE'D HAVE *SAFER, CLEANER WATER?*

NO WAY! HE NEEDED A NEW PLACE TO GET RID OF HIS *RADIOACTIVE WASTE!*

SO COMBINE THAT FACT WITH THE BABY ALLIGATORS, AND WHAT DO YOU HAVE?

AN IDIOT FOR A BROTHER.

THREE MONTHS FROM NOW I'LL UNLEASH MY *ARMY OF GIANT, THREE-EYED, MUTANT ALLIGATOR MEN!* THAT SHOPPING SPREE AT THE ANDROIDS DUNGEON IS AS GOOD AS *MINE!*

I MEANT TO SAY, A *TOTAL* IDIOT FOR A BROTHER! THERE'S NO RADIOACTIVE WASTE IN THAT SEWER! THAT FISH WAS A *FLUKE!*

YOU'LL SEE, LISA. EVERYONE IN SPRINGFIELD WILL WITNESS MY *GENIUS!* BWA-HA-HA-HA!

"GIANT, THREE-EYED, MUTANT ALLIGATOR MEN, EH?"

EXCELLENT!

THREE MONTHS LATER...

EUREKA! I'VE *GOT* IT!

PHEW! I'M AFRAID TO ASK WHAT YOU *DID* IN HERE, LISA. THIS ROOM SMELLS LIKE...

...ROTTEN EGGS!

THE KIND OF ROTTEN EGGS THAT WILL BE ALL OVER YOUR FACE WHEN WE SHOW OUR EXPERIMENTS TOMORROW AT THE SCIENCE FAIR. *HA!*

SO WHAT KIND OF RESULTS DID YOU GET, DR. STINKYPANTS?

IF YOU MUST KNOW, I'VE BEEN ABLE TO *ISOLATE* A LONE *AMINO ACID* THAT COULD HOLD THE *CURE* TO THE *COMMON COLD!*

BY TAKING THESE EGGS, AND EXTRACTING THE PROPER AMOUNT OF AMINO ACID FROM THE DNA STRAND WHILE EXPOSING IT TO HARD LIGHT...

BLAH, BLAH, BLAH! EGG SALAD SANDWICHES FOR EVERYONE ON THE PLANET. WHO CARES? HURRY UP, LISA. IT'S TIME TO CHECK OUT *MY* EXPERIMENT!

DO NOT EAT

GLUE

LOOK OUT, SPRINGFIELD! HERE COMES *BART SIMPSON* AND HIS *MUTANT ALLIGATOR MEN REVIEW! WOO-HOO!*

UNNNGGH! MAN, IS THIS THING SEALED TIGHT! IT WOULD TAKE AN ARMY TO REMOVE THIS.

OR THE FLICK OF A LASER BEAM HYDRAULIC CODE DESCRAMBLER BUTTON.

I'VE BEEN MONITORING YOUR LITTLE EXPERIMENT, BART, AND HAVE COME TO SEE WHAT WE'VE CREATED FIRSTHAND.

MR. BURNS!!!

WHAT DO YOU MEAN, 'WHAT WE'VE CREATED'?!?

YOUR EXPERIMENT WAS CONDUCTED IN MY SEWER SYSTEM WITHOUT MY PERMISSION. SO, IF THERE ARE ANY MUTANT ALLIGATOR MEN UNDER THIS CITY, THEN I HAVE A RIGHT TO THEM, TOO.

ACCORDING TO OUR INTERPRETATION OF THE LAW, WHAT MR. BURNS SAYS IS PERFECTLY TRUE AND LEGAL.

I'LL BE THE JUDGE OF THAT!

CHIEF WIGGUM! WOW! I NEVER THOUGHT I'D BE HAPPY TO SEE YOU!

OKAY, MR. BURNS. LET'S POP THE TOP OFF THIS CAPER!

OHHH, ALL RIGHT. OPEN THAT MANHOLE FOR ME, SMITHERS, AND LET'S GET THIS OVER WITH!

YES, SIR!

CLICK!

71

PHEW! WHAT A *HORRIBLE SMELL!* OKAY, PEOPLE, WHO GOES DOWN *FIRST*? WHO'S MOST *EXPENDABLE*?

VERY FUNNY. OKAY, I'LL GO, BUT *AFTER* THE KIDS.

STILL HAPPY TO SEE HIM, BART?

I'LL SAY. I'VE GOT GUM ON MY SHOE.

THIS IS SO *GROSS*!

KEEP YOUR EYES OPEN. THERE COULD BE MUTANT GATORS LURKING ANYWHERE.

≥GASP!≤ BART WAS *RIGHT*! THIS SEWER SYSTEM IS *FILLED* WITH RADIOACTIVE WASTE FROM THE NUCLEAR POWER PLANT!

CHIEF WIGGUM, YOU'VE GOT TO *DO* SOMETHING!

KEEP KICKING, CHIEF WIGGUM. ALLIGATORS *LIKE* BITING BARE FEET.

HERE, GATOR, GATOR, GATOR. COME TO PAPA.

SEAL IT BACK UP, BOYS. THERE'S NOTHING DOWN THERE TO *THREATEN* THE PEOPLE OF SPRINGFIELD. OUR WORK HERE IS *DONE*.

NO MUTANT ALLIGATOR MEN. PHOOEY! ALL THAT WORK FOR *NOTHING*.

OH, AND DON'T BE LATE AGAIN WITH YOUR DONATION TO THE *POLICE BENEVOLENCE FUND*, MR. BURNS.

BUT WHAT ABOUT THE *NUCLEAR WASTE*? BURNS SHOULD BE *ARRESTED!*

QUIET, LITTLE GIRL!

I STAND CORRECTED. THANK YOU, CHIEF WIGGUM.

THE NEXT DAY...

...THAT *CONCLUDES* OUR STUDENT SCIENCE EXHIBITION EXCEPT FOR BART SIMPSON, WHOSE "RADIOACTIVE ALLIGATOR MEN IN THE SEWER" EXPERIMENT *FAILED* TO SHOW RESULTS, AND LISA SIMPSON, WHOSE *ILLITERATE* FATHER ATE HER "EGGS FOR A COLD-FREE WORLD" EXPERIMENT.

I CAN'T BELIEVE YOU THOUGHT MY SIGN SAID "*DONUT-EAT*" INSTEAD OF "*DO NOT EAT*."

CAN'T YOU TELL THE *DIFFERENCE* BETWEEN AN EGG AND A DONUT?!

AT LEAST DADDY WON'T EVER BE SICK AGAIN.

AND HERE TO PRESENT THIS YEAR'S AWARDS IS THE OWNER OF THE ANDROIDS DUNGEON.

BEHOLD! I HOLD IN MY HAND ENVELOPES CONTAINING *THREE $25 SHOPPING SPREES* AT THE ANDROIDS DUNGEON.

SINCE I *ALONE* WILL CHOOSE THIS YEAR'S WINNERS, I WILL DO SO ACCORDING TO *MY OWN LAWS* AND *SUPERIOR REASONING*.

...*THIRD PLACE* GOES TO *RALPH WIGGUM* FOR HIS "MY DAD'S SHOE IS STUCK TO MY HEAD WITH GUM" EXPERIMENT. I HAVEN'T SEEN ANYTHING SO FUNNY SINCE SPOCK LAUGHED OUT LOUD IN THE SECOND "STAR TREK" MOVIE.

THANKS, MISTER. THE SHOE KEEPS MY HEAD FROM WEARING A SKI CAP!

SECOND PLACE GOES TO *LISA SIMPSON* BECAUSE OF HER *DISREGARD* FOR THE CHOLESTEROL LEVEL OF HER EXPERIMENT AND BECAUSE SHE WILL PROBABLY SPEND HER $25 ON ALL THE *GIRL-FRIENDLY COMICS* I HAVE GATHERING *DUST* IN MY SHOP.

SCIENCE FAIR- SPONSORED BY THE ANDROIDS DUNGEON

...BUT...

OH, LISA, I'M SO *PROUD*, MY ARTERIES FEEL LIKE *FLUBBER*.

AND *FIRST PLACE* GOES TO *BART SIMPSON* FOR *FOLLOWING HIS DREAM* TO CREATE A *NEW RACE* OF SUBTERRANEAN MUTANTS REGARDLESS OF THE *DANGERS TO MANKIND* AND *SUPERHERO-KIND ALIKE*.

HURRY, HOMER! WE'VE GOT AN *ANGRY MOB* ON OUR HANDS!

SMAK!

MY KID SHOULD HAVE WON!

WE WAS ROBBED!

UNFAIR!

74

MEANWHILE, BELOW THE STREETS OF SPRINGFIELD...

COME ON! TIME TO GET UP!

THAT'S IT. COME OUT OF *HIDING*. AND BECAUSE YOU STAYED HIDDEN, THERE WILL *SECOND HELPINGS* AT DINNER TONIGHT FOR ALL OF YOU.

NOW IT'S OFF TO WORK WITH YOU...

I SAY WE GO *UNION*. PASS IT ON!!

...AND DON'T FORGET YOUR *MINING TOOLS*, MY PRECIOUS LITTLE MONSTERS. *BWA-HA-HA-HA!*

THE END

75

THE CASE OF THE MISSING MOON WAFFLES

FROM THE SECRET FILES OF LISA SIMPSON

ONE MONDAY MORNING...

AAIIIEEEE!!! MY WAFFLES! MY *DELICIOUS* MOON WAFFLES!* THEY'RE GONE. *GONE!* SOMEONE *ATE* MY *GLORIOUS* WAFFLES!

LOOKS LIKE THERE'S A *MYSTERY* IN NEED OF SOLVING. IF I COMBINE MY *DEDUCTIVE REASONING* WITH MY *KEEN OBSERVATIONAL SKILL,* PERHAPS THE TRUTH SHALL COME TO LIGHT.

DAD, WHEN WAS THE *LAST TIME* YOU SAW THE ALLEGED MOON WAFFLES.

:SNIFF: :SOB: WELL, LISA, DADDY ONLY LOOKED AWAY FROM HIS PLATE FOR A *SPLIT SECOND* TO CHECK THE *STOCK PAGES,* AND WHEN I LOOKED DOWN AT MY PLATE :WHIMPER: THEY WERE *GONE!*

IT WAS THE BOY! *THE BOY DID IT!*

*TO MAKE HOMER'S PATENTED, SPACE AGE, OUT OF THIS WORLD MOON WAFFLES JUST POUR WAFFLE BATTER, CARAMEL, AND LIQUID SMOKE INTO A WAFFLE IRON. THEN WRAP THE COOKED WAFFLE AROUND A STICK OF BUTTER AND ENJOY!

DON'T LOOK AT ME! I DIDN'T TAKE HIS MOON WAFFLES. I DON'T EVEN *LIKE* THEM.

THE *CARAMEL* GETS STUCK IN MY TEETH AND THE *LIQUID SMOKE* MAKES ME BREAK OUT IN A *RASH*.

MOM, WHERE WERE YOU WHEN THE MOON WAFFLES *DISAPPEARED*?

LISA, I DON'T HAVE TIME FOR *ANOTHER* ONE OF YOUR FATHER'S *WAFFLE CRISES*. I NEED TO MAKE THESE LUNCHES, OR YOU'LL BE LATE FOR SCHOOL.

MAGGIE?...

≧SUCK!≦
≧SUCK!≦

AFTER GATHERING ALL THE *CIRCUMSTANTIAL EVIDENCE* AND WEIGHING ALL OF YOUR *ALIBIS*,

ONLY ONE PERSON COULD HAVE EATEN THE WAFFLES.

IT WAS... *YOU!*

77

YOU'RE RIGHT! IT WAS ME. I ATE THEM, AND THEY TASTED SO GOOD AND CRUNCHY AND TOASTY AND...

AAIIIEEEE!!! MY WAFFLES! MY DELICIOUS MOON WAFFLES! THEY'RE GONE. GONE! SOMEONE ATE MY GLORIOUS WAFFLES!

WAH-HA-HA!

DAD, YOU ATE THEM. REMEMBER? YOU JUST CONFESSED!

BUT HOW DID YOU KNOW?

THREE THINGS TIPPED ME OFF. FIRST OF ALL, YOU HAVE BEEN KNOWN TO FORGET THAT YOU HAVE FOOD IN YOUR MOUTH WHILE CHEWING IT.

SECONDLY, YOU HAVE NEVER READ THE STOCK PAGES IN YOUR LIFE.

AND FINALLY, THE STOCK MARKET ISN'T OPEN ON SUNDAYS, SO THERE IS NO LISTING ON MONDAY MORNING!

I DO SO READ THEM!

BUT WHAT POSSIBLE INTEREST COULD YOU HAVE IN THE STOCK PAGES?

THE COMMODITY LISTINGS. IT'S LIKE AN ALPHABETICAL TRIP TO THE GROCERY STORE. THERE'S BEEF AND EGGS AND ORANGES AND PORK BELLIES...

MMM...PORK BELLIES.

OOO!- PORK BELLIES ON A MOON WAFFLE!

DOUBLE MMM...

THE END

TERRY DELEGEANE
STORY

MIKE WORLEY
PENCILS

SCOTT MCRAE
INKS

RICK REESE
COLORS

KAREN BATES
LETTERS

MATT GROENING
MR. BUTTERWORTH

"ALL'S VELDT THAT ENDS VELDT!"

OUT OF THE *WAY,* FOLKS!

B'WANA BART THE *WILD ANIMAL-HANDLER* COMIN' THROUGH!

WHAT THE--?

OH, *MY!*

FLING!

BRUFF RUFF RUFF! BRUFF RUFF RUFF!

MEOWRRR!!!

SCOTT SHAW!
STORY & PENCILS

PHYLLIS NOVIN
INKS

RICK REESE
COLORS

KAREN BATES
LETTERS

BILL MORRISON
EDITOR

MATT GROENING
HEAD ZOOKEEPER

BART, I *KNOW* YOU'RE EXCITED ABOUT VISITING *STAMPY* AT THE *SPRINGFIELD WILD ANIMAL PRESERVE...*

...BUT PLEASE, *CALM DOWN!*

:WHIMPER!:

BUT, MOM, I HAVEN'T SEEN GOOD OL' *STAMPY* SINCE WE SENT HIM OUT THERE!

HE IS STILL *MY PET!* I *WON* STAMPY IN THAT *CONTEST* ON BILL AND MARTY'S "MORNING ZOO" *RADIO SHOW!*

YEAH, I COULD'VE *KILLED* THOSE STUPID *DISC JOCKEYS* WHEN THEY *GAVE* YOU A FULL-GROWN AFRICAN *ELEPHANT!*

LISA, DO YOU HAVE ANY IDEA WHERE *MAGGIE* IS?

LISA!?!

HUH?

I ASKED YOU IF YOU KNOW WHERE MAGGIE IS!

OH, SORRY, MOM, I WAS BUSY LISTENING TO MY NEW CD BY *"O-ZONE PLAYERZ"!*

I THINK MAGGIE'S IN THE LIVING ROOM WATCHING TV...

♪PORKEYMEN♪... GOTTA PITCH ♪ 'EM ALL...♪

≀SUCK!≀ ≀SUCK!≀ ≀SUCK!≀ ≀SUCK!≀

TODAY, OUR HEROES *COMPETE* AGAINST A TOTALLY *NEW* ASSORTMENT OF WEIRD *CREATURES* WE HAVEN'T EVEN *SOLD* TO YOU...*YET!*

"WHAT'S NEW PORKEYMEN?"

≀SUCK!≀ ≀SUCK!≀ ≀SUCK!≀ ≀SUCK!≀

PIKKA-*BOOGAH!* SNUK-SNUK!

WOOBWOOBWOOBWOOB

WOOBWOOBWOOBWOOB

PIKKA-BOOGAH!

OH, *THERE* YOU ARE! COME WITH ME, MAGGIE...

≀SUCK!≀ ≀SUCK!≀ ≀SUCK!≀ ≀SUCK!≀

WOOBWOOBWOOBWOOB

HERE'S MAGGIE! SHE WAS JUST WATCHING ONE OF HER *CARTOON* SHOWS!

WHEW!

WELL, LET'S *SNAP IT UP*, PEOPLE! I'VE GOT A *PACHYDERM* WAITING FOR ME!

♪ ...LA DE DAH DE LAH...LET'S *RECYCLE* OUR LOVE...IN THE *COMPOST* OF LIFE ...LA DAH DAH *DAH*... ♪

OH, SHE'S JUST IMMERSED IN THAT NEW MUSIC CD OF HERS.

WHATEVER IT IS THAT LISA'S *SINGING* IS DRIVING ME *NUTS*!

YEAH, SHE'S LISTENING TO HER FAVORITE *BOY-BAND* --*THIS* WEEK, AT LEAST!

EFORE TOO LONG...

ALL *RIGHT*! STAMPY, HERE WE *COME*!

THAT RIDE WASN'T SO *BAD*, WAS IT? NOW WE CAN *STRETCH* OUR *LEGS*!

WELL, *START STRETCHIN'*, MARGE!

THE EMPTY *PARKING SPACES* LOOK LIKE THEY'RE ABOUT *THREE MILES AWAY* FROM THE GATE!

SPRINGFIELD WILD ANIMAL PARK

THOSE *ADMISSION TICKETS* COST ME A SMALL *FORTUNE*, SO I'M *EXPECTING* YOU KIDS TO HAVE THE *BEST* TIME OF YOUR SHORT *LIVES*!

OH, DON'T WORRY YOUR SHINY HEAD ABOUT *THAT*, HOMER!

SOUVENIRS AHOY!

WHEW! I NEED TO *FRESHEN UP* IN THE NEAREST *LADIES' ROOM*! HOMER, WOULD YOU PLEASE *WATCH* MAGGIE?

THE HAPPY HUNTER SOUVENIR SHOP

THE GRINNING

MAN, I CAN HEAR THOSE *RUBBER SNAKES* CALLIN' MY *NAME* "BART SSSSSSSIMPSON!"

YOU GET *BACK* HERE, BOY!

SUCK! SUCK! SUCK! SUCK!

PLOP!

81

A FEW MINUTES LATER...

WHAT ARE YOU BOYS DOING IN *HERE*?

AW, MARGE, HE WAS TRYING TO SHAKE ME DOWN FOR A PHONY *TARANTULA*!

I'M JUST CHECKIN' OUT THE *RUBBER SNAKES*!

SOON...

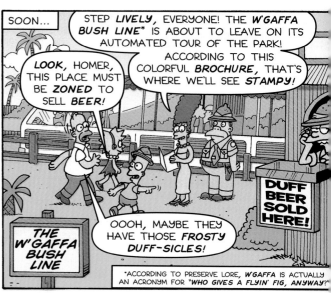

STEP *LIVELY*, EVERYONE! THE *W'GAFFA BUSH LINE** IS ABOUT TO LEAVE ON ITS AUTOMATED TOUR OF THE PARK!

ACCORDING TO THIS COLORFUL *BROCHURE*, THAT'S WHERE WE'LL SEE *STAMPY*!

LOOK, HOMER, THIS PLACE MUST BE *ZONED* TO SELL *BEER*!

THE W'GAFFA BUSH LINE

OOOH, MAYBE THEY HAVE THOSE *FROSTY DUFF-SICLES*!

DUFF BEER SOLD HERE!

*ACCORDING TO PRESERVE LORE, *W'GAFFA* IS ACTUALLY AN ACRONYM FOR "*WHO GIVES A FLYIN' FIG, ANYWAY?*"

WELCOME ABOARD THE *W'GAFFA BUSH LINE*! PLEASE KEEP YOUR HANDS *INSIDE* THE TRAM TO AVOID *FEEDING* THE ANIMALS...YOUR *HANDS*, THAT IS!

MMM...*GAZELLE-ICIOUS*!

OH, *MY*! ISN'T ALL THE *WILDLIFE* SIMPLY *BREATH-TAKING*, HOMER?

WELL, I THINK THEY'RE "BREATH-TAKING", MOM...ESPECIALLY SINCE NONE OF THESE WALKING MANURE-FACTORIES ARE *HOUSE-BROKEN*!

WHOOP! WHOOP!

RAHHHRRWW!

TOOKI-TOOKI!

BLARGHH!

HEY, LOOK...A SLOTH! NOW *THERE'S* AN ANIMAL I CAN *REALLY RELATE* TO!

YEAH, ALL IT NEEDS IS A *COUCH*, A *TV*, A BAG OF *CHIPS*, AND A *SIX-PACK*!

OH, ISN'T THAT BABY *CHIMP* JUST THE *CUTEST* THING YOU'VE EVER *SEEN*? *SOMEHOW*, IT REMINDS ME OF MAGGIE...

...*MAGGIE*!?! OMIGOSH, *WHERE'S* MAGGIE?!?

82

WHAT'S *WRONG,* MOM?

IF YOU WERE PAYING *ATTENTION,* YOUNG LADY, YOU'D *REALIZE* THAT YOUR *LITTLE SISTER* IS *MISSING!*

NOW MARGE! LET'S ALL *MELLOW OUT.* TAKE A *LESSON* FROM THE *SLOTHS!*

DON'T YOU SLOTH *ME,* HOMER! *YOU'RE* THE ONE WHO WAS SUPPOSED TO BE *WATCHING* MAGGIE!

LOOK, MOM, IT WAS *MY* FAULT HOMER LOST MAGGIE, SO I'LL GO *FIND* HER AND BRING HER *BACK,* SAFE 'N' SOUND!

HMMM, I DON'T KNOW IF THAT'S SUCH A *GOOD* IDEA...

DON'T THINK OF IT AS *LOSING* A SON BUT AS *GAINING* A DAUGHTER!

ACTUALLY, I WAS *SAVING* THAT THOUGHT FOR BART'S *WEDDING DAY!*

"WEDDING DAY?" MOM, *PUH-LEASE* DON'T *GROSS* ME *OUT* WHILE I'M ABOUT TO SAVE MAGGIE'S *BACON!*

HOP!

MEANWHILE, MAGGIE'S STILL UNDER THE INFLUENCE OF HER NEW "MASTER", *PIKKANOSE...*

⸭SUCK!⸭ ⸭SUCK!⸭ ⸭SUCK!⸭ ⸭SUCK!⸭

SHE'S THINKS SHE'S ON A *MISSION* FOR HIM!

PIKKA-*BOOGAH!* SNUK-SNUK!

⸭SUCK!⸭ ⸭SUCK!⸭ ⸭SUCK!⸭ ⸭SUCK!⸭

⸭SUCK!⸭ ⸭SUCK!⸭ ⸭SUCK!⸭ ⸭SUCK!⸭

DANGEROUS! KEEP OUT!!!

AT THE SAME TIME...

THIS DIRECTION LOOKS LIKE IT MIGHT BE A *SHORT CUT* BACK TO THE TRAM STATION!

WELCOME
TO THE
AFRICAN VELDT!
(LEGAL DISCLAIMER:
NOT THE AFRICAN VELDT)

OKAAYY...NO PROBLEMS SO FARRRR...EVERYTHING'S COOOOOL...

GRRRRR

GRRRROWWWLLL

YAAAHH!!

:PUFF!: :PANT!: :PUFF!:
:PANT!: :PUFF!: :PANT!:

HEY, HAVEN'T YOU GUYS EVER HEARD OF *"THE CIRCLE OF LIFE"*?

OF COURSE, THAT'S JUST A *NICE* WAY OF REFERRING TO *"THE SURVIVAL OF THE FITTEST"*!

D'OH!

RRROARRR!!!

MAYBE I CAN *LOSE* 'EM IF I CAN JUST *MAKE IT* ACROSS THIS *CHASM*!

LEAP!

GLOM!

SKIDD!

:UNNGHH!:
GOT IT!!!

ERGHHH!

...

HUH?

--STAMPY!?!

¦EEENGHHH!¦

GRAB!

YOU STILL LIKE TO TREAT PEOPLE LIKE HUMAN PACIFIERS, HUH, STAMPY?

STUFF!

THEY SAY ELEPHANTS NEVER FORGET, BUT I'D SURE LIKE TO FORGET THIS! YECHHH!

MEANWHILE, MAGGIE TRIES TO CARRY OUT THE TELEVISED ORDERS OF PIKKANOSE: TO CONQUER ALL THE WILD ANIMALS SHE CAN FIND...

¦SUCK!¦ ¦SUCK!¦ ¦SUCK!¦ ¦SUCK!¦

MAGGIE'S FIRST OPPONENT IS A SILVERBACK BULL LOWLAND GORILLA AND HIS FAMILY...

¦SUCK!¦ ¦SUCK!¦ ¦SUCK!¦ ¦SUCK!¦

¦GRRNK?¦

GROOT! GROOT! GROOT!

WHAP! WHAP! WHAP! WHAP!

¦SUCK!¦ ¦SUCK!¦ ¦SUCK!¦ ¦SUCK!¦

¦SUCK!¦ ¦SUCK!¦ ¦SUCK!¦ ¦SUCK!¦

HURL!

85

MAGGIE'S AIM IS *TRUE*, STRIKING THE GORILLA ON ITS SENSITIVE *NOSE*...

BWOINK!

HUH?

MAGGIE IS *TRIUMPHANT!*

OOH!

SUCK! SUCK! SUCK! SUCK!

OOOOH!

WUG!

OOH!

PLOP!

NOT EVEN THE MIGHTY *CAPE BUFFALO*, THE WORLD'S MOST *DANGEROUS* ANIMAL, CAN WITHSTAND PIKKANOSE-MAGGIE!

SUCK! SUCK! SUCK! SUCK!

SNORRT!

NOR THE FLEET-FOOTED *CHEETAH*, THE WORLD'S *FASTEST* ANIMAL, CAN BEST PIKKANOSE-MAGGIE!

MEORRR!

AND AS FOR THE MYSTERIOUS *PLATYPUS*, THE WORLD'S ONLY *POISONOUS* WARM-BLOODED ANIMAL, IT'S *NO CONTEST!*

SUCK! SUCK! SUCK! SUCK!

SPA FON!

BACK ON THE TRAM...

OH, I'M A *TERRIBLE* MOTHER!

I'M *SURE* THAT *SOMEWHERE* THERE ARE MOTHERS EVEN *WORSE* THAN *YOU!*

86

AS I *RECALL*, MAGGIE *DISAPPEARED* WHILE *YOU* WERE SUPPOSED TO BE *WATCHING* HER!

YEAH, BUT THAT'S ONLY BECAUSE YOU WERE TOO BUSY *"FRESHENING UP"*, AND *LISA* HERE WAS TOO BUSY *LISTENING* TO HER "BOZO PLAYERS" CD!

THAT'S "O-ZONE PLAYERZ," DAD.

UNH, A LITTLE *HELP* HERE?

AT THE RISK OF REPEATING MYSELF...

...HELP!!!

HEY, HOW *ABOUT* THAT--A *TALKING ELEPHANT!*

NO, DAD, IT'S *STAMPY*, AND HE'S GOT *BART* IN HIS *MOUTH!*

OMIGOSH! WE'VE GOT TO *HELP* HIM!

C'MON, FOLKS--LESS *YAKKIN'*, MORE *UNPACKIN'!*

MAYBE I CAN BREAK OFF ONE OF THESE ⦃UHHN⦄ *BRANCHES...!*

AND *REACH* BART WITH IT FROM HERE...

WHOOPSIE!

AAAGHHH!

LISA!!!

MAYBE AFTER YOU *RESCUE* BART AND MAGGIE, YOU COULD HIKE BACK TO THE *REFRESHMENT STAND* AND GET ME A *BEER?*

HONEY, ARE YOU *ALL RIGHT?*

OOF!

YEAH, I *GUESS* SO...

THWUMP!

THERE GOES THE *TRAM!* IT'S *AUTOMATED*, SO THERE'S NO CHANCE OF IT *STOPPING* OR *TURNING BACK!*

⦃AHEM!⦄ A LITTLE *HELP* HERE?

DUST!

DUST!

OH, *SORRY,* BART!

87

C'MON, STAMPY, SPIT OUT BART! *NICE* STAMPY! *GOOD* STAMPY!

UH, I HATE TO *TELL* YOU THIS, LIS', BUT STAMPY IS A *SAVAGE BEAST!*

"SAVAGE BEAST?" THAT *REMINDS* ME OF AN OLD *QUOTATION* "MUSIC HATH *CHARMS* TO *SOOTHE* THE *SAVAGE BEAST!*" WELL, TO BE ACCURATE, THE QUOTE IS "*MUSIC* HATH *CHARMS* TO *SOOTHE* THE *SAVAGE BREAST*...

YOUR *EARS* ARE A LOT *BIGGER* THAN THESE HEADPHONES WERE *DESIGNED* FOR, STAMPY!

CLIP!

WHATCHA *DOIN'*, LISA? YOU GONNA *PUNISH* STAMPY BY MAKING HIM *LISTEN* TO "*THE O-ZONE PLAYERZ*"?

♪ ...LA DE DAH DE LAH...LET'S *RECYCLE* OUR LOVE...IN THE *COMPOST* OF LIFE...LA ♪ DAH DAH *DAH*... ♪

BART! YOU'RE *ALL RIGHT!*

WELL, *I'VE* ALWAYS THOUGHT SO!

EWWW!!! YOU'RE ALL *SLIMY* WITH *ELEPHANT SPIT!*

YEAH! *COOL*, HUH?

SPTOOEY!

LOOK *OUT*, LIS'! I'M GONNA GET *ELEPHANT SLOBBER* ON YOU!

NEVER MIND *THAT*, BART! WE'VE GOTTA FIND *MAGGIE* AND *FAST!*

88

MEANWHILE, A PACK OF *LAUGHING HYENAS* ARE COMPLETELY *IMMUNE* TO MAGGIE'S "PORKEYMEN" TECHNIQUES...

≥SUCK!≤ ≥SUCK!≤ ≥SUCK!≤ ≥SUCK!≤

YEEHEE HEEHEE!!!

HYUK-HYUK-HYUK!

BUT THEY *DO* THINK SHE'S JUST ABOUT THE *TASTIEST-LOOKING* LITTLE MORSEL THEY'VE EVER *SEEN!*

YEEHEEHEE SLURP!-- YEEHEEHEE!!!

YEEHEEHEEHEE!!!

≥SUCK!≤ ≥SUCK!≤ ≥SUCK!≤

≥SUCK!≤ ≥SUCK!≤ ≥SUCK!≤

≥SLURP!≤

≥SUCK!≤ ≥SUCK!≤ ≥SUCK!≤ ≥SUCK!≤

YANK!

SNAP!

89

WHOA, MAMA! STAMP 'EM, STAMPY!

≋HREENK!!!≋

≋SUCK!≋ ≋SUCK!≋ ≋SUCK!≋ ≋SUCK!≋

STOMP! BASH!

YII!! YII!! YII!! YII!! YII!!

BACK AT THE TRAM STATION...

I'M NOT *BUDGING* UNTIL I'M *REUNITED* WITH OUR POOR, LOST *CHILDREN!*

AW, C'MON, MARGE! THEY'LL TURN UP *EVENTUALLY!*

HIIII-YO, STAMPY!

HI, MOM AND DAD! STAMPY *HELPED* US FIND *MAGGIE!*

≋SUCK!≋ ≋SUCK!≋ ≋SUCK!≋ ≋SUCK!≋

OH, MAGGIE, MY SWEET, WONDERFUL LITTLE *BABY!* I'M *SO* GLAD YOU'RE *SAFE!*

≋SUCK!≋ ≋SUCK!≋ ≋SUCK!≋ ≋SUCK!≋

UH, MARGE, I THINK SOME *"TOUGH LOVE"* PARENTING IS IN ORDER!

MAGGIE, YOU WERE A VERY *BAD* GIRL TO *RUN OFF* LIKE THAT! *BAD GIRL, MAGGIE!*

MAGGIE USES HER PORKEYMEN TECHNIQUE ONE LAST TIME...ON *STAMPY!*

DON'T LOOK S... *DOWN* I... THE *MOUTH* HOME! DON'T YO... REALIZE HOW *FEW* PEOPL... EVER GE... TO SEE A... ELEPHANT... *UVULA...*

HEY!

≋ERGHHH!≋

STUFF!

THE END

SIMPSONS COMICS PRESENTS

BART SIMPSON

LITTLE RASCAL

#8

US $2.50
CAN $3.50

APPROVED BY THE COMICS CODE AUTHORITY

MATT GROENING
J.Ho
REESE

©2002 BONGO ENTERTAINMENT, INC. THE SIMPSONS ©&TM TCFFC. ALL RIGHTS RESERVED.

BART SIMPSON... THE TIME HAS *FINALLY* COME...

...TO THROW THE *BOOK* AT YOU.

THE Dickens YOU SAY

AND THE BOOK IS "GREAT EXPECTATIONS" BY CHARLES DICKENS.

YOU DILLY-DALLIED BART, AND ALL THE *OTHER* BOOK REPORT CHOICES WERE TAKEN.

WHUMP!

THIS ISN'T A BOOK. IT'S A *LIFE SENTENCE*.

YOU SHOULD HAVE PICKED EARLY AND GOTTEN A *THIN* BOOK, BART. *I'M* READING "GREAT VICE PRESIDENTS OF THE 20TH CENTURY".

I PICKED "SURVIVING IN THE UNLIKELY EVENT OF A PLANE CRASH."

THE PICTURES ARE *FUNNY*.

I'M NOT GONNA *SWEAT* IT, MILHOUSE.

WHAT ARE *YOU* *TALKING* ABOUT? IT'S DUE *TOMORROW*.

IT'S A *NEW* WORLD WE LIVE IN, MY FRIEND.

THE AGE OF *MULTI-MEDIA*.

SOON...

THE ANDROID'S DUNGEON & BASEBALL CARD SHOP

HOW MUCH IS THAT *CLASSICS ADUMBRATED* COPY OF "GREAT EXPECTATIONS", MY MAN?

THIS COPY?

"TAKE ME TO YOUR COMIC BOOK & BASEBALL CARDS"

YES WE'RE OPEN

THIS COPY IS *SIGNED* BY NONE OTHER THAN HAL KILBY, THE CREATOR OF BUTTERFLY GIRL AND THE EMERALD SQUAB.

HAL KILBY DREW THIS?

TOFUMAN

GREAT EXPECTATION

KID SELTZER

RHINO GIRL

SADLY *NO*. IT ILLUSTRATES THE FOLLY OF SENDING *YOUR* *MOTHER* TO A COMIC CONVENTION TO ACQUIRE AUTOGRAPHS. IT WAS THE *LEGENDARY* SHELBYVILLE COMIC-FEST. I CAME DOWN WITH A CHILD-HOOD ILLNESS AND COULD...

VIGOR COMICS

RADIOO MAN

GREAT EXPECTATIONS

NEE

LONG STORY SHORT. YOU WANT TO *SOAK* ME FOR IT.

A KING'S RANSOM WOULD BE A *MERE* DOWN PAYMENT.

GREAT EXP

≥SIGH.≥

SO MUCH FOR *THAT* PLAN, BART.

I'M DOWN BUT NOT *OUT*, MILHOUSE.

I'VE BARELY *BEGUN* TO SCRATCH THE SURFACE OF THE MEDIA RESOURCES AT MY DISPOSAL.

I NOW TURN TO THE MAN WHO CAN MAKE *ANY* DREAM COME TRUE.

WELL, KIDS, LET'S GIVE A GREAT BIG ROUND OF KRUSTY APPLAUSE TO JACK SAFARI AND HIS CIRCUS OF CARRION EATERS!

I'M *NOT* DEAD!

I TELL YOU I'M *NOT*, YOU FOUL BEAST!

SOMETHING *SPECIAL* NEXT, KIDLETS. IT'S NOT OFTEN WE TAKE *REQUESTS* ON THIS SHOW. BUT ONE LITTLE TYKE CALLED TO TELL ME THAT HE'S ONLY GOT *ONE WEEK* TO *LIVE*.

AND THE *ONE THING* THAT WOULD SEND HIM INTO THE *AFTERLIFE* WITH A SMILE ON HIS FACE WOULD BE HIS FAVORITE *CARTOON*.

WHAT'S A CLOWN TO *DO*?

THIS ONE'S FOR *YOU*, BART SIMPSON.

THIS *ISN'T* GOING TO WORK, BART.

WATCH AND LEARN, LIS. WATCH AND *LEARN*.

94

95

LET ME *GUESS*...

...THAT WAS *NOT* AN ACCURATE ADAPTATION OF THE DICKENS CLASSIC.

HA! HA! HA! HA!

YOU ONLY HAVE A FEW MORE HOURS UNTIL BEDTIME, AND YOU PINNED YOUR HOPES ON A *CARTOON*!

I'LL ADMIT DISAPPOINTMENT BUT *NEVER* DEFEAT!

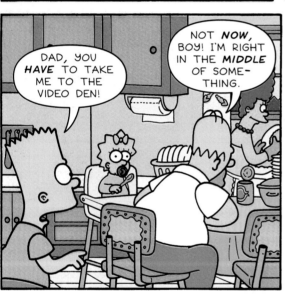

DAD, YOU *HAVE* TO TAKE ME TO THE VIDEO DEN!

NOT *NOW*, BOY! I'M RIGHT IN THE *MIDDLE* OF SOME-THING.

ONE MORE PEA ADDED TO THIS STACK AND I'LL HAVE *BROKEN* MY PERSONAL RECORD.

BUT IT'S FOR *SCHOOL*, HOMER.

YOU *HEARD* HIM, HOMER. IT'S FOR *SCHOOL*.

SURE. *THAT* EXCUSE.

HIS EDUCATION COMES BEFORE *MY* DREAMS.

NO!

VIDEO DEN

RENT ONE STEVEN SEAGAL AND GET THREE SYLVESTER STALLONES FREE.

McBAIN XII

JAWS

YOU CAN'T RENT THIS.

YOU MEAN IT'S *OUT*?

NO. IT'S RATED "R".

WHO *KNEW* THERE WERE SO MANY POLICE DOG MOVIES? WHAT A COUNTRY.

DAD, YOU GOTTA *HELP* ME! THE MOVIE I NEED FOR *SCHOOL* IS RATED "R"!

NO SYNC

WOLF

WE'VE HAD THIS DISCUSSION *BEFORE*, YOUNG MAN.

WE'RE NOT HAVING THAT *FILTH* IN OUR HOUSE.

AW, MAN...

SO, THE MOVIE THE KID WANTS IS FOR *ADULTS*, EH? ANY *NUDITY*?

YEAH. GWYNETH PALTROW.

AW, MAN...

VHS

HO, HO. I HEARD YOUR *LATEST* DODGE WENT DOWN IN FLAMES.

STUPID *RATINGS* SYSTEM.

HOW'S A KID SUPPOSED TO *LEARN* ANYTHING?

OH, I DON'T KNOW... YOU COULD TRY ACTUALLY *READING* THE BOOK.

LIKE *YOU'VE* ACTUALLY READ "GREAT EXAGGERATIONS".

AS A MATTER OF FACT, I *HAVE*.

I'LL BET YOU *HAVEN'T*.

I *HAVE*!

I *READ* IT!

GET REAL.

IN YOUR *DREAMS*.

I'LL *PROVE* IT TO YOU!

HEH, HEH. SPEAK INTO THE HIDDEN *MIKE*, LITTLE SISTER.

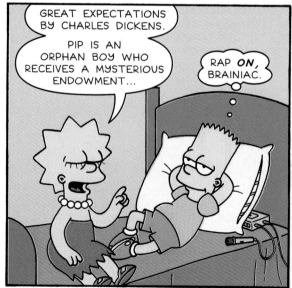

GREAT EXPECTATIONS BY CHARLES DICKENS.

PIP IS AN ORPHAN BOY WHO RECEIVES A MYSTERIOUS ENDOWMENT...

RAP *ON*, BRAINIAC.

TWO HOURS GO BY...

...AND SO WITH THE MYSTERY SOLVED, PIP FACES HIS FUTURE WITH HIS PAST EXPLAINED, AND A LOVE TO SHARE HIS LIFE WITH. THE END.

WHUH?

UH...I GUESS YOU'RE *RIGHT*, LIS. YOU *DID* READ IT.

NOT THAT IT HELPS *YOU* ANY, BART. GOOD LUCK WRITING THAT BOOK REPORT BEFORE *BEDTIME*.

LUCK HAS *NOTHING* TO DO WITH IT.

MAN. THIS IS *MORE* BORING THE SECOND TIME.

BLAH BLAH BLAH BLAH BLAH BLAH...

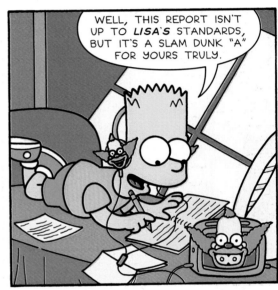

WELL, THIS REPORT ISN'T UP TO *LISA'S* STANDARDS, BUT IT'S A SLAM DUNK "A" FOR YOURS TRULY.

TIME FOR BED, BARTY. I HOPE YOU FINISHED YOUR *HOMEWORK*.

ALL *DONE*, MOM. I HAVE A *GOOD* FEELING ABOUT THIS REPORT.

SO DO I, BROTHER.

SO DO *I*.

99

THE NEXT MORNING...

SO, DID YOU GET THE *REPORT* FINISHED?

IN THE *BAG*, MILHOUSE, MY MAN.

HOW'D YOU *DO* IT? DID YOU GO ON THE *INTERNET*?

NOTHING SO *PRIMITIVE*.

I USED *SUBTERFUGE*.

IS THAT LIKE *RITALIN*?

YOU'RE *NEXT* ON THE LIST, BART.

I HAVE MY REPORT RIGHT *HERE*, TEACH.

"GREAT EXPECTATIONS" BY CHARLES DICKENS.

THIS IS THE STORY OF A GUY NAMED PIP WHO WAS AN ORPHAN. AND WHEN HE GETS TO VOTING AGE HE GETS SENT TO LONDON...

...THAT'S WHERE HE MEETS *JAMES BOND*. EVEN THOUGH HE HAS A *STUPID* NAME, THEY LET HIM BECOME A *SPY* AND HIS FIRST MISSION IS TO *AUSTRALIA* WHERE SOME MYSTERIOUS GUY IS PLANTING BOMBS IN KANGAROO'S POUCHES.

FIVE MINUTES LATER...

...AND SO PIP THROWS MR. BUMBLECHOOK OFF THE EIFFEL TOWER AND THEN MARRIES MOLLY HAVERSHAM ON MTV.

RIGHT ABOUT **NOW**, BART IS FINISHING HIS REPORT BASED ON THAT IDIOTIC STORY I TOLD HIM...

...THE SOUND OF MRS. KRABAPPEL'S RED PEN WRITING A BOLD "F" IS **MUSIC** TO MY EARS.

MUSIC CLASS

WALTZ

THAT REPORT RATES A SOLID "A".

REALLY?

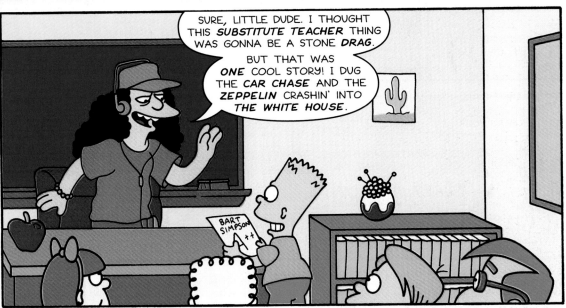

SURE, LITTLE DUDE. I THOUGHT THIS **SUBSTITUTE TEACHER** THING WAS GONNA BE A STONE **DRAG**.

BUT THAT WAS **ONE** COOL STORY! I DUG THE **CAR CHASE** AND THE **ZEPPELIN** CRASHIN' INTO **THE WHITE HOUSE**.

BART SIMPSON ++

THEY SHOULD MAKE A **MOVIE** OF THAT BOOK, MAN!

THEY **DID**. WITH GWYNETH PALTROW.

AW, MAN...

BART SIMPSON A++

THE END

CHUCK DIXON
SCRIPT

DAN DECARLO
LAYOUTS

MIKE KAZALEH
PENCILS

MIKE ROTE
INKS

ART VILLANUEVA
COLORS

KAREN BATES
LETTERS

MATT GROENING
SPEED READER

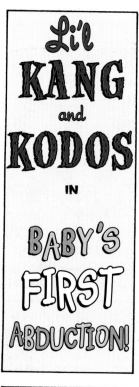

Li'l KANG and KODOS

IN

BABY'S FIRST ABDUCTION!

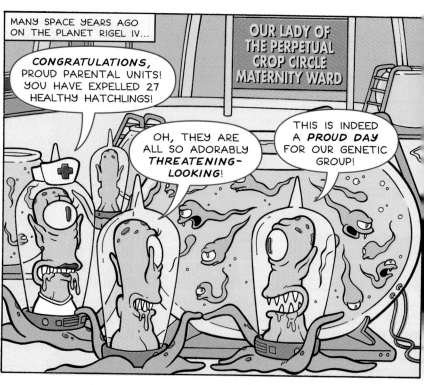

MANY SPACE YEARS AGO ON THE PLANET RIGEL IV...

OUR LADY OF THE PERPETUAL CROP CIRCLE MATERNITY WARD

CONGRATULATIONS, PROUD PARENTAL UNITS! YOU HAVE EXPELLED 27 HEALTHY HATCHLINGS!

OH, THEY ARE ALL SO ADORABLY THREATENING-LOOKING!

THIS IS INDEED A PROUD DAY FOR OUR GENETIC GROUP!

DO YOU HAVE A PREFERENCE?

OOOH. IT IS DIFFICULT TO DECIDE, BUT THESE TWO LOOK PARTICULARLY CRUEL AND BENT ON DOMINATION.

SOMETIMES THEY ARE HARD TO GET IN THE NET.

HERE ARE YOUR PROGENY, JOYFUL COUPLE.

THANK YOU. WILL YOU JOIN US IN THE TRADITIONAL CELEBRATORY FEAST?

AFFIRMATIVE.

SNARF! CHOMP! CHEW! MUNCH! TASTE!

GAIL SIMONE
SCRIPT

DAN DECARLO
LAYOUTS

MIKE ROTE
PENCILS

ANDREW PEPOY
INKS

ART VILLANUEVA
COLORS

KAREN BATES
LETTERS

BILL MORRISON
EDITS

MATT GROENING
TANK CLEANER

EIGHT YEARS LATER, AS THE PRECOCIOUS TYKES GROW UP...

HAPPY 8TH LUNAR CYCLE, KANG AND KODOS!

IT IS JUST WHAT I HAVE MOST DESIRED! *THANK YOU,* PARENTAL UNITS!

BUT *I* WANTED A SPACE PONY!

MY FIRST SAUCER

OH, PLEASE, MAY WE USE THE SAUCER TO ABDUCT SOMEONE, PLEASE, PLEASE, PLEASE?

WELL...I SUPPOSE IT IS ALL RIGHT.

BUT STAY WITHIN ONE MILLION LIGHT YEARS!

WHEEEEEEE!

AHA! HERE IS A PLANET *RIPE* FOR INVASION! NOW WE MUST FIND A SUITABLE VICTIM FOR EXTRACTING *INFORMATION!*

WOOOOOSHHH!*

*YEAH, WE KNOW THERE'S NO SOUND IN SPACE. BUT THEY'RE GOING REALLY FAST!--STAR RANGER BILL

DO YOU THINK THAT THIS CONTAINMENT POD MAKES ME LOOK *FAT?*

THIS EARTHLING SEEMS TO BE SURROUNDED BY *WEALTH.* HE MUST BE THE *LEADER!* LET US ABDUCT HIM!

Monty

103

MRRM...BOBO, MY ONLY FRIEND, MMM...ZZZZZZZ.

HRMMMMMMMMM!

Monty

THE EARTHLING SHOWS NO *FEAR*, KANG! HIS WILL IS *STRONG*!

AH! SO YOU WILL NOT *TALK*, EARTHLING? WELL, WE SHALL SEE ABOUT *THAT*!

ON

THREE HOURS OF TERRIFYING AND CRUEL EXPERIMENTS LATER...

HE IS STILL *SILENT*!

DID YOU TRY THE PROBE? PERHAPS THE PROBE WILL LOOSEN HIS TONGUE. HAVE YOU TRIED THE PROBE?

QUIT ASKING ABOUT THE *PROBE*!

OH, MIGHTY EARTHLING--IT IS *CLEAR* TO US THAT YOU ARE THE *SUPERIOR SPECIES*!

WE NOW RETURN YOU TO YOUR DWELLING. PLEASE DO NOT *KILL US* IN YOUR *WRATH*!

...PERHAPS IF YOU HAD USED A DIFFERENT PROBE...

CEASE SPEAKING OF PROBES IN GENERAL!!!

THE END.

THIS STORY IS DEDICATED TO THE MOST HEROIC *STUFFED ANIMAL* OF ALL! THANKS FROM ALL OF US HERE AT BONGO TO BRAVE, BRAVE *BOBO*!

OH, I'VE BEEN OUT HERE **FOREVER**, BUT THE FISH AREN'T DOING ANY NIBBLING WITH THE BITING AND THE BEING COOKED UP WITH LEMON AND THE TARTAR SAUCE. ᕍDO-HEY!ᕍ FORTUNATELY, I HAVE A FASCINATING **TALE** OF **SCIENCE GONE MAD** TO KEEP MY MIND AND ᕍHOO-HOOᕍ OFF MY **STOMACH** WITH THE GROWLING AND THE EMPTINESS, ALSO! IT'S ANOTHER OF...

PROFESSOR FRINK'S PARTLY PROBABLE PARABLES:

SASHIMI BART!

BART, I JUST WOULD LIKE TO **THANK** YOU FOR HELPING WITH THE WASHING AND SUDSING OF MY NEW **POGO-MOBILE**.

AS YOU KNOW, IT'S THE ONLY VEHICLE TO HARNESS THE AWESOME POWER OF **POGO**.

I CALL IT THE **UP-CHUCK TRUCK**.

SPRINGFIE
INSTITUTE
SCIENCE
DRIVE-THRU OPEN
TIL MIDNIGHT!

YES, AND **I** WISH YOU'D **STOP**. ᕍNG-HEY!ᕍ

GAIL SIMONE	DAN DECARLO	JASON HO	ART VILLANUEVA	KAREN BATES	MATT GROENING
STORY	LAYOUTS	PENCILS/INKS	COLORS	LETTERS	CATCH OF THE DAY

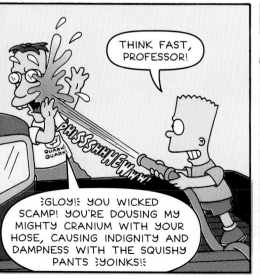

THINK FAST, PROFESSOR!

ᕍGLOY!ᕍ YOU WICKED SCAMP! YOU'RE DOUSING MY MIGHTY CRANIUM WITH YOUR HOSE, CAUSING INDIGNITY AND DAMPNESS WITH THE SQUISHY PANTS ᕍYOINKS!ᕍ

FORTUNATELY, I FORESAW THIS POSSIBILITY AND CREATED ᕍHOO-HA!ᕍ THE **SPLASHBOTS** FOR THE PURPOSE OF REVENGE, HEY!

AAAHHH! GLUB!

DOUSE THE HUMAN CHILD.

AFFIRMATIVE. SOAKING IS PRIME DIRECTIVE.

GOTTA GET SOME COVER... I'LL HIDE IN THE *LAB!*

CORE PROGRAMMING DEMANDS CONTINUED IMMERSION OF HUMAN CHILD!

RETURN FOR ADDITIONAL SPLASHING, HUMAN!

HEH...NEVER GET IN A WATER FIGHT WITH A *SCIENTIST.*

HE'LL BE SAFE IN THE LAB, OF COURSE. THERE'S ABSOLUTELY *NO DANGER*, AS LONG AS HE DOESN'T...

...PUSH THE BUTTON ON MY AMPHIBIAN TRANS-MUTATION MACHINE!

?

OH, FOR THE LOVE OF LIMPET!

BART! YOUR MOTHER IS *STILL* MAD AT ME FOR THAT TIME I *ACCIDENTALLY* TURNED YOU INTO A *PARAMECIUM.* YOU'RE *DELIBERATELY* TRYING TO GET ME IN TROUBLE WITH THE *YELLING* AND THE *LAWSUITS* AND THE CALLING OF *NAMES!*

I'M *SORRY*, PROFESSOR!

SPLASH THE HUMAN!

NOT *NOW*, YOU *IDIOT!*

106

...AND SO WHAT YOU'RE TELLING ME IS THAT MY SON IS NOW A *FISH*?

ER....YES. SORRY.

SAY, IS YOUR WIFE GOING TO BE ALL RIGHT WHAT WITH THE *PASSING OUT* AND *FALLING* TO THE *FLOOR*?

EH. I'LL GET HER A PILLOW LATER.

MAGGIE! DON'T FEED HIM TOO MUCH, OR HE'LL DIE!

WELL, I'M CERTAIN YOU HAVE A LOT OF BREADING AND PAN-FRYING...UH, ER, I MEAN *CATCHING UP* TO DO, SO I'LL JUST LEAVE BEFORE YOUR WIFE *WAKES UP* AND STARTS *HITTING* ON ACCOUNT OF I BRUISE EASILY AND THE *AMBULANCE* CHARGING AN ARM AND A LEG ⨳HOO!⨳

ER...GOODBYE, YES.

SOON...

OH, WHAT A *HORRIBLE* DREAM.

THAT'S NOT LIKE ME, TO TAKE A SIESTA IN THE MIDDLE OF THE DAY, *PARTICULARLY* ON THE LIVING ROOM FLOOR. I'D BETTER GET TO CLEANING THE BATHROOM, AS SCHEDULED!

LESS TALK, MORE SPOCK!

HI, MOM! DAD SAYS THIS IS MY NEW BEDROOM!

OH MY *WORD!*

THE NEXT MORNING...

NO...WE ARE **NOT** SELLING OUR SON TO THE **CIRCUS,** AND THAT'S **FINAL.**

GOOD THINKING, MARGE! WHY LET THOSE **SLEAZY RINGMASTERS** MAKE ALL THE MONEY?

I'M NOT QUITTING SCHOOL TO SELL **CORN DOGS,** DAD! BESIDES, WE **NEED** THAT BATHTUB, SOME OF US MORE THAN OTHERS!

WE'LL JUST CHARGE THE RUBES FIVE BUCKS A POP TO LOOK AT HIM IN THE BATHROOM! LISA CAN SELL CORN DOGS! OF COURSE, SHE'LL HAVE TO QUIT **SCHOOL**...

WELL, I CERTAINLY CAN'T QUIT SCHOOL. I DON'T EVEN **GO** TO SCHOOL!

AWWW, CAN'T I JUST BE A CRIME-FIGHTING FREAK?

THERE'LL BE NO **CRIME-FIGHTING** OR **FREAKISM** IN **THIS** HOUSE, YOUNG MAN!

OH, HOW **ADORABLE!** MAGGIE KISSED BART'S BOWL! GOOD BABY!

BART, I'M **SORRY,** BUT I'M AFRAID YOU'RE GOING TO HAVE TO GO TO SCHOOL JUST LIKE **ANY OTHER** KID.

SMECK!

BUT HOW ABOUT I MAKE YOU A NICE PLATE OF **PANCAKES,** OKAY? THEY'RE YOUR FAVORITE!

UGH...

SIGH: ALL RIGHT, YOU CAN HAVE **WORMS** ON YOUR PANCAKES.

YUM!

108

BART! I ASKED YOU A *QUESTION*. ARE YOU EVEN *LISTENING*?

NICE FISH BOWL, FISH BOWL HEAD. HA, HA!

WELL, IT'S KINDA HARD CONCENTRATING WITH THIS *SEA CAPTAIN* STARING AT ME ALL THE TIME!

HAWLEY SMOOT and YOU

FLOUNDER FACE! FLOUNDER FACE!

I'M SORRY, BART. BUT MY MOM SAYS I SHOULDN'T BE *FRIENDS* WITH A *FISH*! I COULD GET *FIN ROT*!

MAN, THIS STINKS LIKE MACKEREL. WHY COULDN'T I HAVE GOTTEN A *USEFUL* MUTATION, LIKE A SHRUNKEN *HEAD* OR *EARS* THAT THROW *LIGHTNING BOLTS*?

SPROING!!

SPROING!

ARF!

ARF!

BART! THIS IS A MATTER OF *LIFE* OR *DEATH*! THERE'S A CAPSIZED *SHIP* AND THE *FLOODING* IS UP TO *HERE* WITH WATER AND THE ICY COLD. ¦BRRRRRRR!¦

ONLY *YOU* CAN SAVE THE CREW!

WELL, THEN, WHAT ARE WE *WAITING* FOR?

WHOA, DUDE!

AWESOME!

THE ONLY WAY IN IS THROUGH THE *PORTHOLES*, BART, AND THE *RESCUE DIVERS* ARE ALL TOO *BIG*! ¦HOY!¦ TAKE THESE *OXYGEN MASKS* AND FIND A WAY FOR THE CREW TO GET *OUT*!

UH...CAN'T WE THINK THIS THROUGH A LITTLE?

ER, *NO!*

POOT!

WAAUUGHH!

SPLOOOOSH!

LOUSY FRINK. KICKING ME OUT OF THE POGO-MOBILE!

GOOD THING I CAN BREATHE *UNDERWATER*. NOW IF ONLY I CAN FIGURE A WAY TO GET THESE GUYS *OUT*.

THE MINUTES ARE TICKING BY, AS OUR PLUCKY LITTLE *FISH-BOY* IS CAUGHT IN A RACE AGAINST TIME TRYING TO RESCUE THE BRAVE CREW OF THE *S.S. MINI-TITANIC*. BOY, WHAT IDIOT THOUGHT UP *THAT* NAME?

OH, MY SPECIAL LITTLE FISH-GUY!

THERE THEY ARE! HE'S *DONE* IT! HE'S *DONE* IT!

¡GASP!¡

HOORAY! THREE CHEERS FOR BART!

WHOA! WHO KNEW THAT A *BOAT* WOULD HAVE A *TRAP DOOR?*

BART! YOU *DID* IT! YOU SAVED THOSE MEN!

THAT'S NOT ALL, MOM! LOOK AT THIS *OLD CHEST* I FOUND WHILE I WAS DOWN THERE!

BACK AT HOME...

GREAT NEWS, SIMPSON FAMILY! I'VE DEVELOPED AN *ANTIDOTE* THAT'LL CHANGE BART BACK TO HIS OLD RASCALLY SELF. ¡GLAVIN!¡

I'M SURE GLAD THAT *PIRATE GOLD* THAT BART FOUND HASN'T *CHANGED US* AT ALL...

♪ WE'RE *NOT* LISTENING!!! ♪

THE END

BART & MILHOUSE'S ALMOST EXCELLENT ADVENTURE

OH, *MAN!* ANOTHER CRUDDY CLASS TRIP TO A BORING *MUSEUM!* WHY CAN'T WE EVER GO ANYPLACE COOL?

YEAH, LIKE TO A *BROADWAY MUSICAL!*

BROADWAY MUSICALS *AREN'T* COOL!

THEN YOU'VE *OBVIOUSLY* NEVER SEEN *MS. CATHY RIGBY* AS *PETER PAN!*

WHY ARE WE TURNING *HERE?*

WHO'S DRIVING THIS *BUS?*

YOU ARE, OTTO.

YOU HAD ME WORRIED! FOR A MINUTE THERE, I THOUGHT THE *BUS* WAS GOING WHERE *IT* WANTED TO GO!

ARL KRESS
SCRIPT

DAN DECARLO
LAYOUTS

JASON HO
PENCILS/INKS

ART VILLANUEVA
COLORS

KAREN BATES
LETTERS

MATT GROENING
HILLBILLY AT HEART

HEY, BART, WHAT'S A "GENERAL STORE"?

BRUCKER'S GENERAL STORE

I'LL BET THEY SELL *MILITARY STUFF* TO *GENERALS!* MAYBE WE COULD BUY SOME *LEFTOVER NUKES* THERE!

WOW! THINK WHAT *THOSE* WOULD DO TO THE TOILETS AT SCHOOL!

AWW, HECK! IT'S JUST A DUMB OLD STORE LIKE THE KWIK-E-MART!

WELL, THEN LET US HAVE *TWO SQUISHEES*, PLEASE, MY MAN!

SQUISHEES? THE ONLY THING I GOT THAT'S SQUISHY IS A *RAG SOAKED IN TURPENTINE!*

NO, NO, A SQUISHEE IS LIKE *CRUSHED UP ICE* WITH *FLAVORED GOO* SWIRLED IN!

OHHH, YOU OUGHTA TRY OUR LOCAL TREAT, *CHIPPED ICE ON TOAST!* HERE YA GO!

THIS IS *HARD WORK*...AND *COLD*, TOO!

QUIT GRIPING AND AIM FOR THE TOAST!

TINK!

TINK!

CHIPPED ICE ON TOAST! BOY, ONLY A *HALF-HOUR* OUT OF SPRINGFIELD AND EVERYTHING IS *SO DIFFERENT* HERE!

HEY, MILHOUSE, LET'S *DITCH* THIS FIELD TRIP!

NO, BART! OH, MAN! OH, MAN! OH, MAN!

KEEP IT TOGETHER, MILHOUSE! IT'S NOT LIKE THIS IS THE *FIRST TIME* WE'VE DITCHED A DOPEY SCHOOL THING!

IT'S NOT *THAT!* NOW I SEE WHY EVERYBODY LOOKS THAT WAY IN THERE! I LOST A TOOTH ON THAT STUPID CHIPPED ICE! *OW! OW! OW!*

HA, HA, HA! COOL!

CLUNK!

21...22...23...CLOSE ENOUGH! LET'S HIT THE ROAD, OTTO!

FAR OUT!

GRIND!

WHAT DO WE DO *NOW?* WE'RE OUT IN THE MIDDLE OF *NOWHERE!*

I SPY A COUPLE OF *LOCAL YOKELS!* LET'S HECKLE THEM FOR A WHILE!

HEY, *HAYSEEDS!* WHA'CHA UP TO? DOING *HARD TIME* FOR MISSING THE MORNING *HOG SLOPPING?*

ARE YOU KIDDIN', KID? THAT'S MY *SECOND* FAVORITE PART OF THE DAY!

WINK!

I'M MAX AND THIS HERE'S COUSIN SAM, AND OUR *FAVORITEST* GAME TO PLAY IS *THIS* HERE ONE! WE SEE WHO CAN *COVER THE FENCE FIRST,* WITHOUT MISSING A SPOT!

WANNA TRY? T'AIN'T AS EASY AS IT LOOKS, BUT IT SHORE IS *FUNNERIFFIC!*

TOM...HUCK... *THIS* SCAM WENT OUT WITH *VANILLA ICE! I'LL* SHOW YOU HOW TO HAVE *FUN* PAINTING THE FENCE!

SOON...

YOU WAS *RIGHT,* BART! THIS SHORE *IS* FUN!

YEAH! NEXT, CAN WE TRY SOME OF THAT THERE *VANILLY ICE?*

SPLOOP!

SLORSH!

SQUINCH!

SPLAT!

ALWAYS SIGN YOUR WORK, BOYS!

THANKS FOR HELPIN' US FINISH OUR CHORES.

YOU WANNA SAIL OUR BOAT IN THE CRICK WITH US?

THAT'S *KID STUFF!* I'LL SHOW YOU WHAT THE *BIG BOYS* PLAY WITH!

NAILING A *SKATE* TO A *BOARD*? WHA'JA SAY THEY CALLS THAT AGIN?

WHEN *BART* DOES IT, THEY CALL IT "*ART*"!

EAT MY DUST, RUBES!

LOOKY THERE!

GO, BART!

WAL, I'LL BE *HORNSWOG-GLED!*

WHIZZZ!

FLOOM!

CHUNK!

GIVE 'ER A GO, SAM THE SHAM!

:GULP: OKAY, I RECKON!

WHOOZ!

FLORP!

HE *WRECKONED,* ALL RIGHT!

IS I DAID?

YOU *FLEWED,* COUSIN SAM!

LET'S GO INTO THE HOUSE. I'LL SHOW YOU A GAME THAT'S NOT *QUITE* SO DANGEROUS!

SOON, AT A NEARBY TAVERN...

JERKWATER SALOON

HELLO, JERKWATER SALOON...CORNY SPEAKING.

CAN YOU SEE IF *I.M. DAMP* IS THERE?

JUST A SECOND, I'LL CHECK.

I.M. DAMP. *I.M. DAMP!* DOES ANYONE SEE *I.M. DAMP?*

NOT WITH YOUR *APRON ON,* CORNY!

WHY YOU LITTLE DELINQUENT! IF I *EVER* GET MY HANDS ON YOU, I'LL MAKE YOU *PAINT THE BAR!*

HOPPIN' HORN TOADS, BART! YOU *SHORE* KNOWS HOW TO HAVE FUN!

THERE ARE THE BOYS THAT *DEFACED CITY PROPERTY!*

MAYOR

OKAY, SAM AND MAX, TIME TO *PAY* FOR YOUR SHENANIGANS!

BUT HOW'D YOU KNOWED IT WAS *US?*

MAYOR MAYNOT!

116

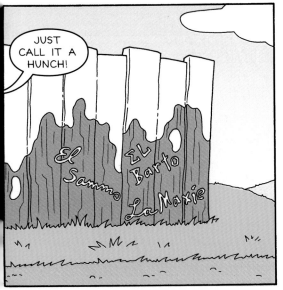

JUST CALL IT A HUNCH!

El Sammo El Barto La Maxie

NOW YOU'RE GOING TO PAINT THE FENCE *AGAIN*... AND *KEEP* PAINTING IT UNTIL *I* SAY YOU'RE DONE!

YES, SIR.

HA, HA, HA! THEY SURE HAVE A THING FOR *PAINT* IN THIS TOWN!

UH, BART...

UH-OH.

YOU KNOW, BART, MAYBE THIS *COULD* BE FUN!

AW, *PIPE DOWN* AND *PAINT!*

EL BARTO

THE END

BART SIMPSON

TRASH THRASHER

MATT GROENING